W. H. Newlin

An Account of the Escape of Six Federal Soldiers from Prison at Danville

W. H. Newlin

An Account of the Escape of Six Federal Soldiers from Prison at Danville

ISBN/EAN: 9783744761260

Printed in Europe, USA, Canada, Australia, Japan

Cover: Foto ©ninafisch / pixelio.de

More available books at **www.hansebooks.com**

"THE TIMES THAT TRIED MEN'S" SOLES.

AN

Narrative of Prison Escape.

BY W. H. NEWLIN,

Late First Lieutenant Seventy-third Illinois Volunteers.

More than Twenty Nights' Travel on Foot.
Six Regiments and Five States Represented.

———•‹FOUR ILLUSTRATIONS, VIZ:›•———

"FOILED AT SEVEN-MILE FERRY."—Page 20.
  "LEFT ALONE."—Page 53.
    "TROUBLE AT LEWIS'S HOUSE."—Page 93.
      "OUT OF THE WOODS."—Page 107.

Also, Memoranda of Three Years' Service of Company "C," Seventy-third Ill. Vol. Infantry, embracing Sketch of part borne by Opedycke's Brigade, in Battle of Franklin, Tennessee, November 30, 1864.

——— FIFTEENTH THOUSAND. ———

AT THE FIRST OPPORTUNITY

After arriving within the Union lines, the author of this *"NARRATIVE"* drew from the Quartermaster's Department, Lytle Barracks, Cincinnati, Ohio, March 31, 1864, the following articles, viz.:

One pair of Pants,	$2 50
One pair of Drawers,	90
One pair of Stockings,	32
One pair of Shoes,	1 48
One Blouse,	3 12
One Overcoat,	7 50
One Flannel Shirt,	1 53
One Cap,	58
	$17 93

John Hutsinpiller was the Lieutenant and Acting Quartermaster. The invoice above was certified as being correct by A. J. Hogan, Captain 1st Ky. Vol. Inf., commanding barracks. I certify now, this June 2, 1888, that I did not draw the clothing before it was needed; and that before getting into it I was relieved of more hair than I have ever been relieved of since, at any one time.

W. H. NEWLIN.

The large, plain, and clear type in which this *"Narrative"* appears makes it well adapted for reading while riding in a railway passenger coach.

From a letter lately received, I take the liberty to quote as follows:

"WASHINGTON, D. C., May 27, 1888.

"MY DEAR MR. NEWLIN:

"I have been in Washington City since sending the photograph to you from Cincinnati. Been busily occupied with portraiture among the denizens of this beautiful city. Came via the Chesapeake & Ohio Railroad—going from Cincinnati to Winchester, Ky., then striking the trunk line, on through Ashland, Ky., Huntington, Va., to Charleston, Kanawha Falls, and up the New River. What grand scenery! O my! Carried your book along and kept myself interested in what you saw and felt in that rough and mountainous, but now—in peace—charming country. Since coming East, have spent four days at the Summer home of Mr. George Alfred Townsend (Gath), at Gapland, Md. He has 130 acres in the very center of Crampton's Gap, where the battle of Crampton's Gap was fought September 14, 1862, three days before the battle of Antietam. . . . I painted a sketch from the famous Burnside Bridge. . . . Shall yet send for a number of copies of your story. Very truly your comrade, with best wishes,

"S. JEROME UHL."

To show the success a canvasser has met with, we quote from two letters as follows:

"ANACONDA, MONTANA, April 13, 1887.

"W. H NEWLIN, Danville, Ill.:

"SIR,—I write again, as I think it is about time to order more books. I came here this A. M., and sold twenty-one copies of '**Prison Escape**,' at 35 cents each. Could have sold more, only it rained, and I had to quit work. I am glad your book sells so well Send me 300 copies, by freight, at once to Missoula, Missoula County, Montana. * * "

Same canvasser, in answer to inquiry received, responded substantially as follows:

"BUTTE CITY, MONTANA, March 24, 1887.

"C. C. Doss, Fulda, Minn.:

"SIR,—Your letter of March 12th received to-day. The book, '**Narrative of Prison Escape**,' is printed and bound at Cincinnati, Ohio; and W. H. Newlin lives at Danville, Ill. Would advise you to write to him for prices. I began with the book last Winter by buying twelve copies, and so far I have sold nearly two thousand copies. . . .

"Very truly, LUCY YOUNG."

AN ACCOUNT

OF THE

ESCAPE OF SIX FEDERAL SOLDIERS

FROM PRISON AT DANVILLE, VA.:

THEIR TRAVELS BY NIGHT

THROUGH

THE ENEMY'S COUNTRY TO THE UNION PICKETS

AT GAULEY BRIDGE, WEST VIRGINIA,

IN THE WINTER OF 1863-64.

BY

W. H. NEWLIN,

Lieutenant Seventy-Third Illinois Volunteers.

CINCINNATI:
WESTERN METHODIST BOOK CONCERN PRINT.
1888.

Entered, according to Act of Congress, in the year 1870,

BY W. H. NEWLIN,

In the Office of the Librarian of Congress, at Washington.

PREFACE.

THE account contained in these pages was first written in 1866. Its publication was delayed in the hope that we should learn something of our two comrades who were left behind. After revising and abridging it somewhat, it is presented to the reader in its present form. We were compelled to rely on memory in preserving for publication the incidents here narrated, as while on our trip we had neither pencil nor paper. That reliance, however, was not in vain, as the scenes through which we passed, though here poorly portrayed, are of a character not easily forgotten. They are indelibly enstamped on the memory, and it seems each year as it passes renders the recollection of them more vivid and distinct. It is not needful to state the motives which prompted this compilation. Much of the same character has been written and published, but as this differs in one essential particular, at least, from all that has yet appeared, we hope that fact will form a sufficient excuse for introducing it to the public.

W. H. N.

This Narrative DULY AUTHENTICATED by SWORN STATEMENTS of Two Comrades who were on the Escape, is on file in Pension Claim, No. 352,023.

 After Seventeen Years Inquiry.

From all the information ever obtained touching the fate of first comrade left behind, the *reasonable* conclusion is that he PERISHED at or near the place where we left him, his remains being found and decently buried near Blue Ridge Mountain. Whatever his *fate* may have been, it was *self* decreed. His reasons for preferring to be left alone were satisfactory to him, and were not *all* disclosed to us. One explanation of this last rather singular circumstance may be found in the fact that the comrade was an Englishman, and had been in this country but a few weeks before enlisting.

How much we should like to see the old "darky" to whom we said, "Put your ear to the string-hole," and on his compliance with the request we pronounced the word "*Yankees*." (See page 60.) "I'll git my trowserloons on."

In the case of leaving the second comrade, as described on pages 72-76, there was no option or time for deliberation. The exigencies of the hour compelled a separation. Mr. Tripp succeeded in escaping the notice of our pursuers, though hid in their immediate vicinity, and hearing their talk enumerating reasons for their failure to "*take us in.*" After several days and nights of wandering and hiding, and of varied and interesting experience, Mr. Tripp was recaptured, sent to Richmond, kept there until September, 1864, was paroled, exchanged, and discharged. He is now living near Burlington, Kansas.

John F. Wood died June 20, 1864, "of wounds received in action." Referring to this, Sutherland, in a letter written not long since, says: "What a pity Wood had to die so soon after escaping prison. But he might have died a slow and miserable death at Andersonville had he not escaped."

Sutherland is living in Michigan, near Eagle Station. Smith resides at Dundee, same state. Mr. Smith very narrowly escaped drowning at Craig's Creek. Mr. Sutherland's opportune landing on the opposite bank of the rushing stream barely in time to extend to Smith a helping hand is all that saved him. In addition to all others, we had the perils by "*Bogus Yankees*" to encounter or avoid. We *risked* our lives to save them, and saving them we *risked* them again and again for our country. Having been captured in our third battle, by escaping, at least two of us, added to the three, thirteen more. But all this was better than Andersonville. We *might* have been numbered among the MARTYRS of the nineteenth century. "I would not make that trip again," said Smith, "for the whole state of Michigan," adding "unless I had to."

DANVILLE, ILL., November 27, 1885.   W. H. N.

INTRODUCTION.

IN those "stirring times," during the late war, when powder, and ball, and the bayonet were the orders of the day, an escape from prison and a secret, hidden march through the Confederacy, was accounted an exciting, as well as a very lucky event. Even at this day, accounts of such are not stale, but possess a thrilling interest, especially to those who participated in them and to their friends. Our journey over mountain and valley, over hill and dale, and across rivers, branches, and rivulets almost innumerable, was accomplished mostly in the night time.

We had neither map nor compass to guide us. The north star alone served us in shaping our course, and very often it was concealed by ominous clouds. We took many needless steps, and made many needless and weary miles in consequence of lack of knowledge of the country and of the course we were steering. Sometimes the desolate hour of Winter's midnight found us far from the public highway, and almost inextricably involved in the brush and tangled mazes of the forest. At such times, being almost at our wit's end, we would try to advance on a "bee line" until the open country or some road was reached.

At one time, when much bewildered in the shadowy woods, in night time, we began to despair of success. We sat down to contemplate our condition and our cheerless prospect. Had an enemy been approaching us we could have well-nigh welcomed him, so he brought deliverance. At length the stillness and thick darkness of the night made our loneliness oppressive, and we groped on. Soon we found a road, and realized that the "darkest hour is just before day."

Knoxville, East Tennessee, was the point at which we first aimed, but on nearing the line of the East Tennessee and Virginia Railroad we learned Longstreet's forces were in Bull's Gap. We then bore northward.

On first setting out on our trip we were extremely cautious. During the first nights and days, after starting, we talked only in whispers. We passed houses with the utmost care, as dogs were at almost every house, and their acuteness in discovering our presence was astonishing, in view of the caution we exercised. Early in our trip, one night near eleven o'clock, as we were nearing a house, a dog barked savagely at us. Instantly the front door opened, and by the light of a fire in the fire-place we saw a woman in her night clothing, watching us pass. Late one night, after midnight, we met a citizen on the road. He was on horseback, moving slowly along. He gave the road, at the same time checking his horse slightly. When he had passed by, the way he made his horse scamper was lively, to say the least. "He must be after the doctor, the way he goes," observed Trippe. "He took sick mi'ty sudden," rejoined Wood. "The sight of us at this time is enough to make him sick," put in a third. We were walking in Indian file, and had our blankets drawn loosely over our shoulders and dragging almost on the ground. Doubtless we were scary looking objects, especially as Smith had his bed-quilt hung over him. Thinking the man had possibly gone for re-enforcements with which to "gobble" us, we hurried forward.

The night of our discovery of the cavalry horses, being much wearied, and feeling we were going to be "hard pressed" for food, we climbed into a corn field to hunt for corn that might have been left on the stalks. Each of our party followed two rows across the field and two back, but not a "nubbin" could be found. Not finding a grain of corn on two dozen rows, and the corn blades being also gone, we concluded, as Taylor observed, "They gather their nubbins clean in the Confederacy." "Yes," added Wood, "they can't hold out much longer."

Another night, at a late hour, after Taylor and Trippe had fallen by the way, when in Craig or Alleghany county, we reached a point where the road we were traveling crossed a pike. On reaching the pike we halted, and a disagreement arose among us as to the course we should take. We quarreled, words ran high, and we seemed to have forgotten our safety depended on secrecy, as there was no lack of emphasis in what we had to say. At last Sutherland ended the dispute by saying to me, "Let's go on." We started immediately, leaving Smith and Wood muttering. For more than an hour we steadily pursued our course, when, discovering it was nearly day, we halted in the woods, near the road side, to see if our comrades were coming up. Soon they came along the road, and one of them said, "They'd better not advance too far without support." "Yes," said Sutherland, "we are waiting for the reserves to come up." Soon after we were hid for the day.

The Union people, the hardy mountaineers of Virginia, or those of them with whom we came in contact, rendered us valuable assistance. Without their aid, indeed, and the aid of the negroes, we could hardly have escaped through the almost barren country of the enemy, especially in the inclement season. We have heard from David Hepler, James Huffman, and Mrs. Mann since the war closed. In a letter from Hepler, received not long since, he says: "I have not forgotten the time I came to you in the woods and found you all asleep."

We copy one of Huffman's letters in part. It was dated November 11, 1867: "As to information concerning your fellow-prisoner that was lost the evening you came to my house, it was not the Botetourt Guards that fired on your squad. It was the furnace company. I saw a lady, living near the furnace, who saw the men returning. They said they neither killed nor captured any of your squad. As to Paxton, he is living yet; so are the people that had the boy hid under the bed."

Our latest information respecting Trippe is a report that he was recaptured, taken back, and shot as an example. Of Taylor, nothing has ever been heard, by us at least, and our painful conjecture is that he never reached the lines. Of our three comrades who reached the lines, Smith and Sutherland are living in Michigan, and Wood is supposed to be a resident of the Key-stone State. Smith, of the Fourth Michigan Cavalry, was present at the capture of the Confederate President, Jefferson **Davis.**

A STORY OF THE WAR.

CHAPTER I.

CAPTURE—PRISON AT RICHMOND—AT DANVILLE—SMALL-POX—HOSPITAL AND CONVALESCENT CAMP—WARD-MASTER AND NURSES—ESCAPE FROM THE GUARDS—TRAIN OF CARS—FOILED AT SEVEN-MILE FERRY—NARROW ESCAPE—HIDING IN CAROLINA—CROSSING DAN RIVER—SINGING AND DANCING—EATING AT MIDNIGHT—SABBATH DAY RETREAT—PROVISION EXHAUSTED—EFFORT TO PROCURE SUPPLIES—ITS FAILURE—HARD MARCHING—HUNGER AT MIDNIGHT—HIDING PLACE—WASHINGTON'S BIRTHDAY—SLEEP.

THE writer hereof was among the prisoners captured by the enemy in the battle of Chickamauga, Georgia, September 20, 1863. Others of the regiment to which I belonged also fell into the enemy's hands. As we had served together through all the vicissitudes of a soldier's life in the camp, on the march, and in battle, we resolved to remain together, and stand by each other as prisoners as long as circumstances would permit. On the day after the battle, September 21st, we were placed on board the cars at Tunnel Hill, and sent under a strong guard, by a circuitous route, through Georgia and the Carolinas, to Richmond, Virginia. We arrived in Richmond on September 29th, eight days having been occupied in the transfer of prisoners from the battle-field. We remained in Richmond through the month of October, and until November 14, 1863, when we were removed to Danville, Virginia, which is south-west of Richmond about one hundred and fifty miles, in Pittsylvania county. The transfer was by rail, and each member of our squad succeeded in getting aboard the same car. Near noon of November 15th we reached Danville, and were immediately introduced to our new quarters. Our squad was allotted a space on the second floor of Prison No. 2, a large frame building, where it remained unbroken until December 15, 1863.

A short time previous to this date the small-pox had made its appearance among the prisoners. On December 14th I was taken sick, the usual symptoms of small-pox appearing in my case; and on the 15th I was examined by the Confederate surgeon and sent to the hospital, in company with three other patients from other prisons in the vicinity.

As I here separate from the six persons with whom I had been associated since my capture, and with whom so much discomfort and inconvenience and so many privations had been borne, I here give their names. They were John Hesser and John North, of Company A, Seventy-Third Illinois Infantry Volunteers, and James Kilpatrick, of Company B; Enoch P. Brown, John Thornton, and William Ellis, of Company C. They were all of the same regiment with myself, and the three last named were of the same company. The two first named and myself were all of our squad that lived through the term of imprisonment. My term, however, did not last as long as that of the others, as the following pages will show. If my information is correct James Kilpatrick died as a prisoner under parole early in 1865, at Wilmington, North Carolina. E. P. Brown and John Thornton died at Andersonville, Georgia, in September, 1864. Brown died on the first anniversary of his capture, September 20th, and Thornton died a few days before. William Ellis died at Charleston, South Carolina, near the close of the year 1864. Hesser and North were among the last of the Andersonville prisoners that were exchanged and sent North.

On arriving at the small-pox hospital I was placed on a bunk in Ward No. 1. I kept in-doors for the space of five or six days, at the end of which time I was classed among the convalescents. On or about December 22d, three convalescents, of whom I was one, accompanied by only one guard, went into the woods on the right bank of Dan River, in quest of persimmons. We went some distance into the country, probably four miles, and secured a quantity of persimmons, which we distributed to the patients in Ward No. 1 on our return to it in the evening. While out on this ramble through the woods, guarded by only one person, I was favorably impressed with the notion of attempting an escape from the Confederates at some future time, when strength would permit. The idea was suggested to my mind by the carelessness of the guard, who more than once set his gun against trees and wandered some distance from it.

About Christmas a row of eight wall tents was put up on the hospital grounds, to be used as quarters for convalescents. I was one of eight persons assigned to tent No. 1, and, as I was a non-commissioned officer, the hospital steward placed me in charge of the sixty-four men occupying the eight tents. It is needless to recite here what the duties were that belonged to my position, but I discharged them as faithfully as I could, so as to keep out of the prison-house in Danville as long as possible.

Sometime in the month of January, 1864, the nurses in each of the three wards of the hospital escaped from the guards, and started for our lines. This necessitated another detail of nurses for the wards, and the detail was made from among the convalescents. The hospital steward did me the favor to appoint me as ward-master of Ward No. 1, giving me the privilege of selecting those who were to assist me as nurses in the ward. I selected those with whom I had become most intimately acquainted as convalescents. Lucien B. Smith, of Company F, Fourth Michigan Cavalry; William Sutherland, of Company H, Sixteenth United States Infantry; Watson C. Trippe, of Company H, Fifteenth United States Infantry, and John F. Wood, of Company G, Twenty-Sixth Ohio Infantry, were the persons selected. After a short time, Robert G. Taylor, of Company G, Second Massachusetts Cavalry, was added to our force of nurses, to make the burden of labor in the ward a little lighter on us. We attended the patients in Ward No. 1 day after day, and night after night, as well as we could with the scanty supplies of medicine and food furnished by the Confederates, until the night of February 19, 1864. Very many of our fellow-prisoners came under our care while we were acting the part of nurses. Many of them died, and we saw their bodies carted away to the burying-ground and deposited in their last earthly resting places.

By the 12th of February the small-pox had begun to abate. As a consequence, the convalescent camp and Ward No. 3 were discontinued. A day or two later and Ward No. 2 was cleared of patients and its doors closed. Those who had been attending as nurses were returned to prison. Two weeks, or three at most, could hardly elapse before the hospital would be entirely broken up. In this event we should be returned to the dreary prisons in Danville, whence escape was scarcely possible. To be kept in prison many months, perhaps until death alone should bring release, was an unwelcome prospect, and we looked upon it with feelings of dread. We had friends and comrades among the prisoners, whom we disliked to leave behind us, but as our presence with them could do neither them nor us any good, we determined to improve the first opportunity of attempting an escape from the Confederates, and avoid the prison entirely.

February 19, 1864, was a cool day for lower Virginia, and we would have deferred our escape for a few nights had we not luckily and accidentally ascertained that we should be sent into prison on the morning of the 20th. Our careful, though hasty, preparations for slipping off from the guards were accordingly commenced just before dark on the evening of February 19th. Before entering upon the detailed account of our escape and subsequent trip to the Union lines, it will be requisite to describe briefly the hospital buildings and surroundings.

The hospital was situated one mile south-west of Danville, on the right bank of Dan River. The river runs in a north-east course, consequently the hospital was on the south of it. There were three wards at the hospital, each capable of accommodating fifty patients. The wards were numbered one, two, and three. There were also a cook-house, a steward's office, and a dead-house. These buildings were constructed of undressed pine lumber. Ward No. 1 was located on the top of a high round hill; near its south-east corner, and almost adjoining it was the cook-house. A few steps north of the ward, and equidistant from its eastern and western extremities, stood the steward's office. At the west end of the ward was the dead-house. About one hundred yards south-west of the dead-house Ward No. 2 was situated, on the hill-side. At the foot of the hill, nearly one hundred yards south-west of Ward No. 2, stood Ward No. 3. Directly east of Ward No. 2, and south of Ward No. 1, was the row of tents which had been used by convalescents. Still further east, at the foot of the hill, was a considerable branch, coursing its way northward to Dan River. Just across the branch, on its right bank, was a large wall tent, in and near which all the clothes washing for the hospital was done. The persons detailed to do the washing slept in the tent. The Confederate surgeon in charge of the hospital had his quarters in Tent No. 1 of the row of tents formerly occupied by convalescents. His tent was nearest the cook-house and Ward No. 1. The tent we occupied, when not on duty in the ward, stood just south of the surgeon's tent, and so near it that the ropes supporting it interlocked or crossed those which supported the surgeon's tent. In Ward No. 1 was the receptacle or place of deposit for all clothing that had been washed. Quite a lot of clothing, belonging in part to patients in the different wards, but mainly to the unfortunate ones who had died, was stored away for the use and benefit of those who might be insufficiently clothed. Wards No. 1 and 3 had been whitewashed, but Ward No. 2, which had been put up between them, at a subsequent date, was not.

Near Ward No. 3, at the base of the hill, was a spring of water, from which the hospital was supplied. Between the wards and other hospital buildings, and all about over the hill-sides, stood tall and straight pines. To the north of the hospital, about three-quarters of a mile distant, was Dan River, with its swift, noisy waters, hedged in by steep, rugged banks. To the south-east and south were cleared lands, traversed by a branch and its tributaries. Still farther south were heavy woods, with one point of timber projecting some distance northward, into the cleared land toward the hospital.

During the afternoon of February 19th, William Sutherland and myself were wheeling wood on a wheelbarrow from Ward No. 3 to Ward No. 1. Having to wheel it up hill it was a wearisome task, and we occasionally stopped for rest. Near four o'clock in the evening, while resting about half-way up the hill-side, Sutherland said to me, "It looks to me very much as if this hospital would be broken up soon." I agreed with him in his opinion, and remarked that our lease of time at the hospital was growing short. After a little further conversation, we resolved to consult with the other nurses on the propriety of attempting an escape, and get them to set out with us for our lines on the next night.

In less than an hour's time we had finished our task of wheeling wood, and were resting on our bunks in the tent. Before either of us had met with our comrades, Smith, who was off duty that evening, came to us and informed us he had something to tell us that we would not like to hear. We told him to acquaint us with his news, however unwelcome it might be. We readily conjectured what it was that so interested Smith, and our conjecture proved correct. He had overheard some of the guards in their talking, and had learned that it was the purpose of the Confederates to send us to prison in the morning. This news did not surprise us, and we were heartily pleased to learn the intentions of the Confederates, although they were not of an amicable nature. We resolved to prevent, if possible, the carrying of these intentions into effect. Smith was then told of the resolution we had formed an hour before to set out on the next night for the Union lines. The sun had already disappeared behind the hills. We knew our fate if we remained at the hospital until its light should again break forth in the east. Our purpose to attempt at least, even if we did not succeed, to leave the hospital, the sick, the Confederate guards, and the Danville prisons that night was immediately and firmly fixed.

Our preparations were at once commenced. We were obliged to exercise the utmost caution in all our movements, as a few of the guards were standing about over the hospital grounds; some of them were in the cook-house. We wished by no word, or look, or act of ours, to lead them to suspect our purpose of eluding them and striking for liberty.

Smith left Sutherland and me in the tent and joined Trippe, Taylor, and Wood, who were on duty in the ward. Smith soon found an opportunity of conferring with his associates, and telling them of the meditated escape. Taylor and Wood were anxious to join it, but Trippe, who had but recently recovered from the small-pox, was distrustful of his strength; and as he had once before escaped, and got some fifty miles away, only to be recaptured and brought back, he did not so readily sanction the project. The nurses who were on duty in the ward now, assisted by Smith, gave their exclusive attention to the sick; they were even more attentive than usual. No one would have suspected from their conduct that they would ever forsake the sick ones under their care.

Just before dark Sutherland suggested the propriety of determining on a place of rendezvous for our party after the guards were passed, as it was certain we could not all pass out at once without being seen. I stepped outside the tent, and walked leisurely up hill, and stood near the south end of the cook-house. Directly south of me, about a mile distant, was a prominent point of timber, projecting northward from the main body toward the hospital. This point of timber seemed suitable for the purposes of a rendezvous, and on returning to the tent I directed Sutherland's attention to it. He concurred with me as to the fitness of the place for a rendezvous, and went to the ward to call the attention of Smith, Trippe, Taylor, and Wood to it. As it was important that our party should fix in the mind the place of rendezvous before it was too dark to see, those who were engaged in the ward came out, one at a time, and glanced across at the point of timber. By so doing misunderstanding and delay, at the critical moment, would be prevented. While Trippe was out taking a look he noticed two or three guards approaching him. He walked on down hill in the direction of the wash-house, as if going after clean bed-clothes or other clothing for patients.

Near eight o'clock, P. M., Sutherland sought an interview with the cook, but found the Rebels had not yet left the cook-house for their own quarters; so he quietly withdrew from the room. The cook—who of course was one of our own men—followed him to the door and asked if any thing was wanted. As the Rebels were within hearing, Sutherland answered, "There is a man in the ward who would like to have a little soup, but I guess he can get along without it. If he must have some," continued Sutherland, "I will come back and let you know."

"All right," answered the cook.

Soon after the guards went to their quarters, which were situated near the guard line, but little more than a quarter of a mile distant, south-west of the cook-house. The cook was again sought by Sutherland, and this time he was found alone, and just ready to retire for the night. Sutherland lost no time in making his business known to him. Six haversacks, the best that could be found in the deposit for clean clothing, were delivered to the cook, who agreed to fill them with the best provision the cook-house at the time afforded. Sutherland then busied himself in selecting clothing for our party from the deposit of clothing that had been washed and stored away. When he had selected the number of garments required he carried them down to our tent. He and I then took off the clothing we had long worn, and put on entirely clean suits. We then went to the ward and relieved our four associates, who immediately went down to our tent and put on clean suits also. The six haversacks, which were filled with the best provisions the cook could provide, were brought to the tent from the cookhouse.

Near eleven o'clock, P. M., our arrangements for leaving were about complete, or as nearly so as was possible with the means at command. Taylor, Sutherland, and Wood, each had an overcoat and blanket; Smith had an overcoat and a large bed-quilt. Trippe and I each had a blanket; we had no overcoats, but we wore an extra shirt and blouse apiece. For our feet we provided the best shoes that could be found about the hospital, and took pains to secure long and strong strings for them. During our attendance in the ward, patients about dying, or near death, had in several instances presented the nurses with their overcoats. These overcoats had been sold by the nurses to the guards for Confederate scrip. In this way we had obtained near two hundred dollars in scrip to carry with us on our journey. Taylor had a watch which was in time-keeping order. He also had a canteen. Smith had a half-moon tin bucket, which held about three quarts. The only knives we had were made of sheet-iron.

We had watched in the ward, and perfected our arrangements for leaving by turns, until near midnight. A little after eleven o'clock we waked up two or three of the stoutest patients in the ward, and told them our departure was near at hand, and that they must watch in the ward for us, and keep the lights burning until morning. We then bid them good-by, cast a last glance over the sick, and closed the door of the ward behind us for the last time. We repaired immediately to our tent and completed our final preparations for the trip.

As our tent was near that of the Rebel surgeon we were obliged to carry on our conversation in a low tone. We put our blankets in a convenient shape for carrying, and made everything ready for starting. It was settled, in the first place, that we should slip out from the hospital grounds two at a time. Which two should go first was the next question that came up for decision. Six small sticks were prepared, and we drew cuts. These sticks were of three different lengths, and the two who held the short ones were to pass out first. The two who held the sticks next shortest were to follow in a given time, and the two holding the longest sticks, in due time, were to bring up the rear. When the drawing was over Sutherland and I held the short sticks.

As time was precious we placed our haversacks and blankets under our arms and stepped outside the tent. We stood a moment at the tent door, listening for the voices or footsteps of the guards. No sound fell upon our ears save that of the wind blowing through the tops of the tall pine-trees. On starting we went to the top of the hill and stopped at the south-east corner of the cook-house, where we again listened intently, but heard nothing. The moon, which had been shining at intervals since night-fall, had become partially obscured by floating vapor clouds. We kept our haversacks and blankets under our arms in such a shape as to imitate closely a bundle of clothing. We then walked slowly down the hill toward the wash-house. We followed the path leading to the wash-house until we reached the branch. Instead of crossing the branch on the foot-log we turned to our right and went directly up stream, stepping sometimes on the ice and breaking it. We kept close to the bluff, and stooped slightly, so that it screened us from the west. To our left, on the east of the branch, was a flat or bottom, covered with pine shrubs and other bushes, which hid us from view in that direction. Unless the sentinel on duty had happened to be near the branch while we were passing, we could scarcely have done otherwise than escape unseen. At length we had proceeded, with much caution, a sufficient distance in the direction of our appointed rendezvous to feel light-hearted and secure. We pushed forward rapidly, crossed two rail-fences and gained the shelter of the woods, where we were to await the coming of Smith and Taylor, who had held the sticks of medium length at the drawing a few moments before. Sutherland and I laid our haversacks and blankets aside, and quietly, though anxiously, awaited their approach.

While waiting, after the anxiety and excitement of the moment had somewhat subsided, we found the weather quite cold. Our whiskers became stiff and whitened with frost, and the winds penetrated our clothing. The moon shone out brightly. The sky was without a cloud. Those which had partially covered it, only a few moments before, had cleared entirely away. Our patience was severely tried, as our comrades, so anxiously expected, had not joined us. On getting quite cold in the breezes of the wintery midnight, we danced about on our feet, and extended our arms to quicken the circulation of the blood, and get ourselves warm. In this manner we passed some two or three minutes, when we stood still to listen for the coming of Smith and Taylor. We listened anxiously, but the sound of their welcome footsteps did not greet our ears. "Can it be that they have been caught?" we asked ourselves.

"If they have been caught the Rebels will soon miss us, and be on the alert, searching for us," said Sutherland.

"Perhaps we had better be off then," I answered.

We listened a moment longer, but heard nothing. We then gathered our haversacks and blankets, and started westward through the woods. We had gone but a few steps before we heard the noise of persons climbing the fence. We halted and remained perfectly still, as we were not sure the rebels were not on our trail. Soon we could distinguish the forms of two persons in the moonlight. They were moving toward the point of timber we had just left. We now knew they were Smith and Taylor, and soon had the pleasure of hearing our names called in low, subdued tones by their familiar voices. Our whereabouts was soon made known to them, and they were soon with us. Smith and Taylor wished to know why we had not stopped in the point of timber, as agreed upon. We told them we had stopped there, had waited some time for them, and had given them up as lost, and then started on our journey alone, getting as far as that before hearing them.

We had not long to wait for Wood and Trippe. They had followed Smith and Taylor more closely than the latter had followed Sutherland and myself. When Trippe and Wood had joined us, we introduced ourselves as Federals, and late nurses at the small-pox hospital near Danville, Va. As the squads of two each had formed a junction, our party of six was ready to move.

After adjusting our haversacks and blankets about us, so that we could easily carry them, we set out through the woods in a westerly direction. In the woods we found that the snow which had fallen a few days before had not melted. We disliked to walk on it, as we left a distinct trail behind. We pushed on, however, and soon struck a wagon road, from which the snow had either blown off or melted away. It was not a public road, but was used merely as a timber road, to get out of the woods with loads of rails and wood. Its surface was very hard and gravelly, and we followed it a mile or two in a southerly direction without leaving many distinct foot-prints.

The railroad leading from Danville, Va., to Greensboro, N. C., was soon reached, and we followed it in a south-west course: we walked on the ties, and made very good time. Soon we had reached a part of the road which ran over a high grading. On hearing a distant rumbling noise in the south, we judged there was a train of cars coming. In a few minutes more we saw the head-light on the engine as it came around the curve made necessary by the hills. We quickly slipped down the side of the grading into the bushes, and watched the train as it passed. But one person on the train was visible to us, and that was a man standing at the door of the last car with a lantern in his hand.

On regaining the top of the grade, we resumed our travels, walking on the ties as before. We followed the railroad until we had gone about five miles from our starting-point, when we came to a wagon road, which crossed the railroad at right angles. This road had the appearance of being much traveled; by turning to our right and following it, we went north-west — the direction we wished to go. As we passed a house near the road side, Trippe recognized the place as one he had seen when out before, making his first attempt to escape. He also knew the road we were following would lead us to the Seven-mile Ferry. This ferry was so called from the fact of its being seven miles up Dan River from Danville. We wished to gain the left or northern bank of Dan River before daybreak, if possible, and we pushed on eagerly and rapidly. The road was smooth. Its white sandy surface could be plainly seen. Dense woods, with thick bushy undergrowth, closely lined it on either side. The hill leading down to the ferry was at length reached. It was a long, but not a steep hill. The road as it led us down the hill-side was meandering in its course.

When we were but little more than half-way down hill, the thought that there might be a guard at the ferry happened to suggest itself to Trippe's mind. He proposed that we should retire into the brush near the road side, and wait until he should go on toward the ferry and reconnoiter. We assented to this proposal, and went a dozen steps or more from the road and halted. Trippe went on down hill alone. He was gone several minutes, a half hour almost it seemed to us in our restless anxiety and concern. We became impatient for his return, and quitting our places in the brush, walked down hill on the road. Near the foot of the hill we saw Trippe slowly retreating from the ferry. He had seen us, and removing the cap from his head, was excitedly motioning for us to halt. We stopped immediately,

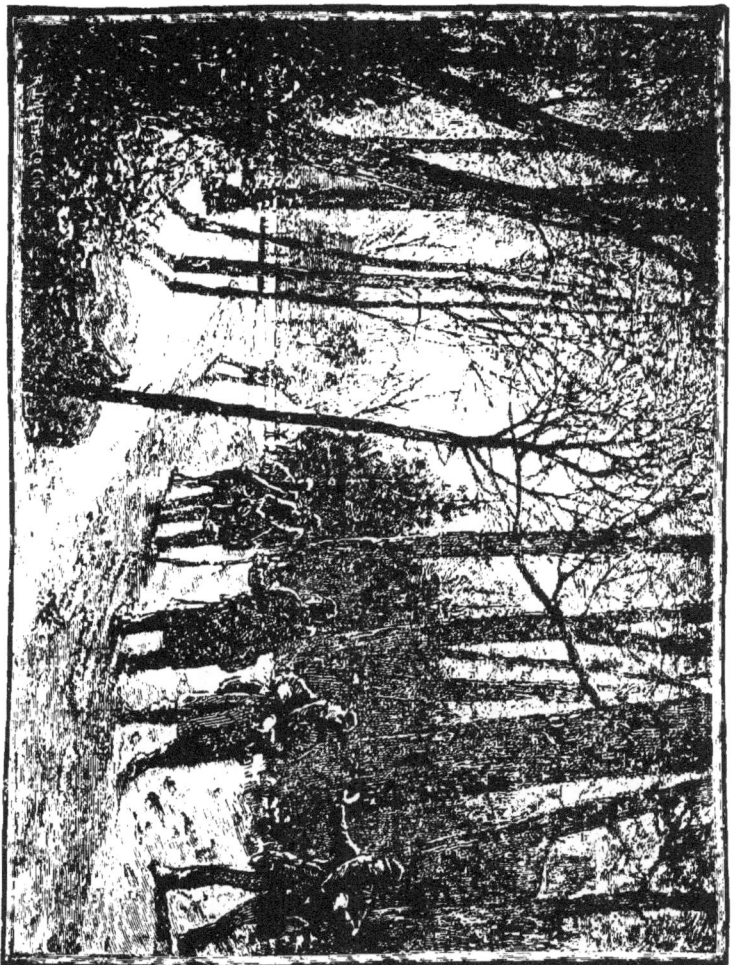

"FOILED AT SEVEN-MILE FERRY."—Page 20.

and kept still. Trippe also stopped, and turned around, looking anxiously toward the ferry. He looked only for a moment, and then quietly rejoined us where we had been waiting. He whispered to us, saying, "Let's go back up hill." We turned about, and walked silently up the road. No word was spoken until we had reached the hill-top. It was to us a moment of deep and thrilling interest and expectancy.

On reaching the upland we halted at the road side, and Trippe reported the discoveries he had made at the ferry. He had gone very cautiously down hill, and had soon stood where he could see the river plainly, and also the ferry-boat. He had stood perfectly still until he had assured himself that no guard was near. He could see nothing but the forest-trees, the river, and the ferry-boat, in the light of the brightly shining moon, which made the frost and waters sparkle. He could hear no sound, save those of the swiftly running waters, and these amply sufficed to drown any noise he himself might make. He turned around and started back to us, to beckon us forward. Almost at the same instant he heard a noise. Thinking he might have trodden on a stick and broken it, thus making the noise himself, he proceeded half a dozen steps further; when, still hearing something, he stopped, and again looked in the direction of the ferry. A little to the right of it, in the edge of the woods, he saw the sparks of a fire flying upward. He watched the fire closely, and it sent up a blaze which shed light far around. One Butternut cavalryman was first seen to stir the fire, and then add fuel to it. Soon three others got up from their bed and warmed themselves. Trippe stood still, and watched them, until they laid down and covered themselves in their bed. He then silently withdrew, feeling sure he had not been heard or seen. As he did so, the horses of the cavalrymen neighed, and pawed the ground, as if manifesting uneasiness. As we were sure the Confederates were not aware of our presence, we felt glad we had escaped so well. Our escape was a narrow one, however; had we arrived at the ferry ten minutes sooner, we should most certainly have been recaptured.

Our disappointment in not getting across the river at the

ferry was great, as we could make no progress in the direction we wished to go until we had gained its northern bank. We consulted briefly as to the course we should pursue; and soon determined to retrace our steps until we should find another road, or some path that would lead us up the river. We started. As the weather was cold and morning approaching, we hurried on. An obscure road, leading off in a south-west direction, was soon found. We changed our course, and followed it. It led by some plantation houses. We left the road and houses some distance to our right, as we did not wish to alarm the dogs and set them to barking.

On returning to the road, we followed it directly up the river until we had traveled five or six miles, from Seven-mile Ferry. It became evident that day-break was at hand. A safe hiding-place for the day next engaged our attention, and we halted. It was first determined that one of our number should go a quarter of a mile further up the road, to see if any houses were near in that direction. Sutherland went some distance ahead, and on returning reported none. As we had passed but one house since falling back from the ferry, we judged we were some distance from any human habitation. The query then arose, shall we hide in the open woods on our left, or in the inclosed woods on our right? After a short parley, we concluded to secrete ourselves in the inclosed woods. We could then get to the river without having the road to cross. Any parties of cavalrymen that might be out scouring the country, were also less likely to come across us in our retreat. Accordingly we crossed the rail-fence, and left it and the road directly behind us. We worked our way through the thickets of brush and briers until we were fully a quarter of a mile from the road, in the direction of the river. On a spot of ground entirely surrounded by pine-trees and bushes we made our bed, and, lying down, soon fell asleep.

The weather being quite cold in the early morning, we waked up at sunrise, on account of cold feet and general discomfort of body. Trippe got up and took a partial survey of the adjacent woods. He went northward, still further from the road we had left at day-break, and found an open space where we could make our bed in the sunshine. To this open space, which was covered over with tall dead grass, we moved our haversacks and bedding. As we wished to rest well during the day, we took pains to make a good bed. Quite a lot of dead grass and leaves was first gathered. On the grass and leaves we spread the four overcoats belonging to our party. On the overcoats we spread Smith's bed quilt. Our caps, haversacks, and blouses were used as pillows, and our five blankets were used as covering. In this manner we usually made our bed all through our trip, varying it, of course, according to circumstances. Having completed our bed, we laid ourselves down to rest, and slept comfortably until late in the day. We made it a rule for each of our party to sleep as much as desired during the day. We did not require one of our number to keep awake as a watch for the others during the day. If we had done so, we, of course, would have watched by turns. The propriety of so doing was often discussed, but we generally deemed it safest to have no watch, as the person watching would have to sit or stand up, and would thus expose himself to the danger of being seen by somebody who might be passing, and so lead to our recapture.

It was near four o'clock in the afternoon of February 20th, when we aroused ourselves from our first slumber as refugees from prison. We got up and went down into a hollow near us, where there was running water, and washed our faces. After combing our hair, we opened our haversacks, and were about commencing to eat, when we discovered that our corn-bread was frozen. Our matches—of which we had two small boxes—which we had luckily procured some two weeks before, now came in good play, as it was needful to have a small fire in order to thaw our bread. We secured a small lot of dry pine limbs and twigs, and built a fire in the hollow sufficient for our purposes; and soon we had dispatched our first meal since leaving Ward No. 1. After finishing our meal, we put our blankets and other baggage in traveling order. As it was too early to set out, we engaged in conversation, laying plans and expedients for effecting a crossing of the river. We resolved to put ourselves across Dan River that night, or on the following day, at almost any risk. As a final preparation for the night's marching, we each secured a stout stick or cane. One of the boys alleged our canes would be needed in case of attack. Taylor had a very large cane for a man of his size. On being spoken to concerning it, he remarked that he was going to cross the river on it. The evening wore away. The king of day having sunk below the western horizon, we began to look for the moon, whose light was to shine upon our pathway. It had not appeared above the horizon; soon afterward, however, the moon arose, and began shedding light. We felt a kind of loneliness on leaving the place which had sheltered us during the day.

As Danville, Virginia, was within one mile of the southern boundary of the State, and as we were at least thirteen miles south-west of that place, we knew we were in the friendly brush and thickets of North Carolina. On setting out, instead of going directly back to the road, we traveled parallel with it for more than a mile. We then changed our course and went back to it, thinking it late enough to travel it without meeting any one. We had gone but a few miles on the road, and passed but one house, when the noise of the river assured us it was not far off. We then left the road and sought the banks of the stream. We crossed an old field, in which we found much mud and water. The walking was slavish and wearisome, as the wet, clayey soil adhered to our shoes. The snow, which had recently melted, had swollen the branches. We found it necessary to cross a branch or almost go back on our trail. By means of a fence, a water gate, and some rails, we succeeded in crossing it without much difficulty. It required time and close watching, however.

On leaving the branch behind us we climbed a fence and entered the woods. These woods were dense, and there was a thick, brushy undergrowth, which greatly impeded our progress. We found it impossible to go directly to the river. It was quite dark, for, although the moon was shining brightly, its light penetrated the heavy woods imperfectly. From the incessant roar of waters we judged we were near the river; but we struggled on through vines and thickets for a full half-hour longer. It was not a great while until we could see, ahead of us, quite an opening; it was the course of the river through the forests. We pressed on and soon stood upon the bank, against which dashed the angry waters. Huge pieces of ice were borne swiftly down the swollen stream. We had thought of constructing a raft of poles and rails, lashing them together with bark and vines; but such materials were not at hand, and the condition of the river forbade the attempt at crossing on a raft. We longed to get across the river, but the prospect seemed all but hopeless.

We pushed on up stream, hoping to find suitable materials for building a raft and a place where the condition of the river would admit of launching it. We had gone a mile or more without discovering any means by which we could cross the stream; still we did not despair; hope continued to struggle against reality. We must get across the river that night, we thought, or venture too far and risk too much to-morrow. The current of water became more rapid and impetuous as we advanced; the roar of the river sounded much louder than before, and our chances of getting across did not seem to improve. We soon came to a drift of logs, slabs, and rails, but owing to the condition of the stream, the quantities of ice and other obstructions in it, we concluded it would be time and labor lost to make a raft and attempt a crossing there. Our resolution to follow on up stream, keeping close to the water's edge until morning, was then fixed. If we failed to find a canoe or other means of crossing before that time we were then to resort to other measures to get us out of our difficulties.

After our minds were fully made up as to the course we should pursue we traveled about two and a half or three miles, when Sutherland and I, who were considerably in advance, espied a canoe fastened to the shore with a chain and padlock. We were almost overjoyed at the discovery. We could not wait for our associates to come up, but followed back down stream to meet them. They were soon informed that we had found a canoe, but they were almost incredulous. In a few minutes, however, all doubts were removed, as they beheld with their own eyes the object of our anxious and careful search. We felt as jubilant and hopeful as if deliverance from all our troubles was just at hand; but, in the excitement of the moment, we did not forget to exercise caution. It was evident the canoe had not been used for several days; the oar was lying in it, frozen in the ice, which had thawed but little; the ice near the middle of the canoe, where the oar was lying, was about three inches thick. In loosening the oar and breaking the chain which secured the canoe, much noise would be made. It was necessary to have two or three rails or poles. Smith and I went out some distance from the river to procure them, and to see if any house was near. We found an old orchard, inclosed by a dilapidated fence. On the southern borders of the orchard we found two log huts, but they were old and tenantless.

We returned to the river carrying with us three or four stout rails. As we were satisfied we should not be heard we set to work regardless of the noise we made. We found the canoe was locked or fastened in a large slab of ice, which extended beyond it into the swift water. We first used our sheet-iron knives and some sharp-pointed and sharp-cornered rocks, and loosened the canoe from its icy bed. A passage-way for the canoe was next broken through the ice to the current of the stream. We then took our stoutest rail and broke the chain by prying on it. I took a rail and placed myself in the end of the canoe farthest out from the shore. Our haversacks, coats, and blankets were then placed in it, and Trippe and Taylor came aboard. Trippe, with the oar in hand, launched us out into the river. We found a swiftly rushing current, and were compelled to row up stream. We kept bearing to our right, however, and soon came in contact with the ice, which extended out from the opposite bank. I took my rail and began breaking the ice. Soon I had broken a narrow passage-way for the canoe, into which we thrust it, and it became steady. I kept on breaking the ice and pushing the pieces aside. The canoe was pushed nearer and nearer the bank. Soon I could reach the low branches of a tree, which stood near the water's brink. I held on to the boughs of the tree, and walked ashore on the ice. Taylor and I removed our baggage from the canoe to the bank. Trippe went to bring over our three comrades, who had been patiently waiting and watching. He found some difficulty in entering the passage way as he neared the bank upon which they stood. In due time our party was safely landed on the shore, for which we had been anxiously striving the best part of two nights.

The first great obstacle to our journey was surmounted. We felt freer and safer. We were several miles from Danville — at least twenty. It was past midnight. The sky above us was perfectly clear. The moon was high in the heavens, and sent down rays of silvery light. Northward, in the direction we wished to travel, the country appeared clear of timber, and we had hopes of finding a good road before going a great distance. When we were ready to leave the river this question arose: what shall we do with our canoe — tie it up or allow it to float down the river? We felt gratefully, even tenderly toward it. It had done us a great service. We concluded to lash it fast to the tree, whose branches hung low upon the bank. We did so; and left it and the river behind us.

We pushed due northward across the cleared fields. Some houses were soon discernible in the moonlight, not far ahead of us. Turning a little to the left, we soon reached a point directly west of the houses. We heard much noise, and stopped to see if we could make out what it meant. We approached a few steps nearer, and heard singing and dancing. We thought it late for such exercises; but as it was Saturday night all was explained, that night being known in Carolina as negroes' night. As we had provisions enough for a meal or two, we did not interrupt the exercises, or make our presence known to the negroes. Nor did we tarry long, as we had no time to lose. We were in Carolina, and had many miles to travel and many weary marches to make through a bleak mountain country before our escape was made good. Our circuit around the houses was continued at a safe distance, until we struck a road running south-east and north-west. We turned to our left and followed the road north-west a little more than a mile. As we felt somewhat hungry, we halted among some bushes at the road side and eat a few pieces of corn-bread. After eating, we pushed on, feeling much refreshed. In a short time we came to a cross-road, when we changed our course and went due north. In that direction we traveled until day-break. A safe hiding-place for the day was next in order, and we set about finding it. We went into the woods some distance to the left of the road, where we found quite a cluster of cedar bushes, in the midst of which we thought we could safely spend the Sabbath day, February 21st. Our bed was at once made and we gladly laid ourselves down to slumber soundly.

It was near three o'clock in the evening when we awoke. On looking about us in all directions, and seeing nobody, we got up. We ventured to a branch, nearly a hundred yards distant, and washed our faces. The canteen and bucket were filled with water and brought near where we had been sleeping. Our toilet was completed by combing our hair, after which we sat down and eat the last of our provisions. How we should procure another supply became the subject of discussion. Various plans were proposed; one of which we determined to try. If it failed we were, of course, to resort to another. The late hours of the evening were passed in adverting to the good fortune which had attended us so far on the trip. The possibilities and probabilities of the future were also alluded to.

As we became deeply interested in our talk the time passed quickly. The tall forest-trees cast long shadows over us. The sun was disappearing in the west. The sky was cloudless. Our preparations for the third night of travel were complete. Soon after dusk we emerged from our hiding place, and in due time were upon the road. Our rest during the day had been refreshing, and we walked briskly forward. We passed one house early in the night. It was too early, we thought, to try our plan for procuring food, and the appearance of the house and its surroundings did not justify the belief that the occupants had any food to spare. So we passed on. Near ten o'clock we came to another house on our left. It was near the road, not more than twenty yards distant. From appearances all inside were asleep. At least no light was visible, and silence reigned. At most of the houses we had passed, the dogs had barked at us. It was not so at this one. We went a few yards beyond the house and halted in the road. Five of us were to lie in wait, while the sixth went forth on the errand of necessity. Which one of us should go upon the errand was a question for decision. It was decided by drawing cuts. Taylor was chosen to attempt the experiment. Taylor's overcoat was of a light-gray color, and had once belonged to a Confederate soldier. Smith's cap was also of "secesh" antecedents. Taylor donned them both, and was to play the Confederate soldier on furlough. He was to go to the front door of the house and knock. When the door was opened to him, if he was asked to come in he was to decline on the pretext of not having time. He was then to apply for something to eat, enough for himself and two comrades a supper that night and breakfast the next morning, which would suffice for one meal for our party. He was to insist on immediate compliance to the request on the plea that he and his comrades were hungry and obliged to march all night. If asked why so? he was to answer that, they had been home on furlough, that their time was nearly out, and that they must report to the company by a certain time—we had anticipated many questions that we judged would be asked, and had answers to suit.

After we had drilled Taylor for a few minutes at the road side, and found him to be a hungry soldier, with nothing Confederate about him except his overcoat and cap, he started to the house. Our eyes followed him as long as he could be seen. We then retired from the road to the fence and waited about twenty minutes, until Taylor returned and made report. He entered the yard in front of the house and approached the door. Before reaching the door his heart suddenly failed of its purpose. He felt himself unequal to the emergency. He immediately turned to his left to examine a smoke-house or other out-house, in which he hoped to find something that would do to eat. The door was securely fastened, which fact caused him to suspect there were some provisions inside. The house was constructed of round logs, and Taylor reached his arm through the space between them to see if he could feel any meat. He examined carefully on each side, but his arm was too short. He could feel nothing. In the mean time, his attention was attracted to another out-building, and he went to examine it. He passed the dwelling, leaving it between him and the road. His search was still unfruitful.

While examining the second out-house he noticed a stable or shed about sixty yards distant. By going to it he would be still farther from the dwelling, and he would feel safer while prosecuting his search. As a last resort before going to the dwelling, he visited the stable in the hope of finding some corn, upon which we would have subsisted in preference to running too great a risk in procuring more palatable food. He could find no corn in the stable, nor grain of any kind. There was some hay or straw, and a lot of corn-blades tied in bundles. In a shed adjoining the stable were six or seven horses feeding on corn-blades. Taylor was impressed with the idea that they were cavalry horses, and on farther examination a saddle or rig for each of the horses was found. He then determined not to visit the dwelling at all, as it was certain there was half a dozen or more men, perhaps cavalry-men, inside of it, sheltering for the night. He then quietly rejoined us at the road side. We had run a great risk; our escape had been narrow. Had Taylor gone half a dozen steps nearer the house he would have walked on some plank or slabs in front of the door; his footfalls might have been heard by those inside, and his presence become known. It was manifest that good fortune was still a companion of our journey. Had the plan we had devised been followed our recapture would certainly have ensued.

It was yet early in the night—near eleven o'clock—and we determined to put several miles between those cavalry-men and our stopping-place in the morning. Before starting, however, we held a short parley as to the propriety of taking the horses and riding them until day-break. On the question of taking the horses our party was about equally divided. The views of those who opposed the project prevailed. The chief objection to it was the great and necessary risk, at the time, in getting the horses to the road without disturbing their owners, and that in case we were retaken, and found guilty of horse-stealing or other depredations, it might go hard with us. By the light of the moon we discovered we had made numerous foot-prints in the road. We could not obliterate them without taking time, and leaving even plainer traces behind us. So we walked backward several yards on the road. On the north of the road were open woods. We stepped aside from the road a few yards and walked parallel with it, face foremost, through the woods, where we could make no tracks. On going about a mile we crossed to the opposite side of the road. In so doing we went south, but left tracks in the road as though we had gone north. We walked rapidly through the woods near the road until we had gone another mile, which brought us to fields. As the walking was not good in the fields on account of the moist clay, we took the road and hurried forward. At short intervals we went on the double-quick. By midnight we had traveled ten or eleven miles. More than one-third of the distance had been gone over since we had found the cavalry horses. Our speed had been accelerated by that discovery. We were much wearied, and halted at a fence near the road side to rest. We were hungry, and would have eaten something, but our haversacks were empty, and hanging loosely at our side. Our rest was brief, but sufficiently long to stiffen our knee and ankle joints.

Our journey was resumed, and we trudged on slowly at first, but soon increased our speed. There were but few houses near the road, and these we passed with cautious steps. A second attempt to get rations was not made that night, as we were fearful of making a second failure, and losing time besides. We resolved to wait until the morrow, and trust to luck or Providence to feed us. The road improved as we advanced, and we made good progress. It bore a little north of west. On crossing a branch we halted and took up some water in our half-moon tin-bucket and drank freely. We then filled our canteen and bucket with water and carried it with us. We were exceedingly tired, and did not wish to take the time and trouble to look out for a hiding-place convenient to water. The gray light of morning was faintly appearing in the east, and we knew our journeying must cease for a time. Our sense of hunger had subsided, or been overcome by weariness. We left the road and went some distance south of it into a heavy forest. When nearly a mile from the road we halted, and quickly spread our bed upon the ground. We then sank wearily to rest, and were sleeping soundly before sunrise.

It was on the morning of February 22d that we had thus sought repose in the wintery forest of Virginia. We had got out of Carolina soon after crossing Dan River, and had traveled almost due northward until we passed Martinsville, Henry county, Virginia. We passed about two miles to the right of Martinsville, and then bore a little west of north. On February 22d we were hid not many miles—probably not more than a night's march—from the southern boundary of Franklin county, Virginia. It was the anniversary of Washington's birth. We remembered the fact, and revered the memory of Washington, although his native State had tendered us a very poor and meager hospitality, and was treating us shabbily. The forest of Virginia, however, protected us from her own and our country's enemies.

CHAPTER II.

SLEEP DISTURBED—NOISE IN THE WOODS—ITS CAUSE—NEGROES FURNISH FOOD—WE HIDE NEAR THE TRAIL—HOUNDS AND HORSEMEN—EXCITEMENT OF THE CHASE—WE BUY A QUANTITY OF PROVISIONS—OUR OBLIGATIONS—ON THE HIGHWAY IN DAYLIGHT—UNDER DIFFICULTIES—WOOD CHOPPER—WOMAN AND DOGS—WE PASS ROCKY MOUNT C. H.—INSECURE HIDING-PLACE—CHANGE OF BASE—WE COME ACROSS A CITIZEN—HE TAKES STEPS TO CATCH US, BUT IS TOO SLOW—OUR FLIGHT—OUR ESCAPE—RUN INTO A WAGON TRAIN—HID AWAY—MAKING MUSH—SNOW—SORE FEET AND LAMENESS—TAYLOR FALLS BEHIND—TAYLOR LEFT ALONE—HIS CONDITION.

WHEN the sun was nearly an hour high, we were aroused from our slumbers by a loud and incessant racket in the woods. We did not uncover our heads at first. A squad of cavalry-men was the first thing of which we thought, but on uncovering our heads and raising up on our elbows, we found it was the noise of wood choppers that had disturbed us. We looked all around us, but could see nobody. The chopping continued, and from the noise we judged several axes were being used. We at once concluded that a party of negroes were at work not far from us, and that we would have an opportunity of procuring supplies. The prospect pleased us. Had we known our conclusion was correct we should have been in an ecstasy of gratitude.

About one hundred yards south of us was a high ridge extending east and west. East of us, about seventy yards distant, was another ridge or spur putting out due northward from the main ridge. We judged from the sounds that the wood choppers were east of us and the ridge last described. By consent of our party, Sutherland and I got out of bed and walked eastwardly to the ridge, striking it not far from the point where it was lost in the level ground. We then crept along on our hands and feet, keeping close together so that we could talk to each other and be understood without speaking loudly. Soon we got around the point of the ridge to a thicket of brush, where we halted. We could see the colored folks at work, plying their axes vigorously. We waited and watched anxiously a few minutes, to see if any whites were with them. We saw none, and were glad of it; we returned to our comrades and made report. We were in a blissful state of mind, and comforted ourselves on the cheering prospect before us. Our feelings no doubt were similar to those of weary travelers in the desert on approaching an oasis.

Our determination to consult with the negroes, and make overtures for food and such other assistance as they could give, was soon made. It was agreed that Sutherland and I should go upon this delicate mission. We went, and soon reached the point from which we had watched the negroes before. We again watched them closely, and assuring ourselves that no whites were near, we emerged from the thicket, and walked briskly toward them. As we approached one of the negroes noticed us. He immediately called the attention of the others to us. Instantly all chopping ceased, and quiet succeeded. At the same moment we halted, and Sutherland put his hand to his mouth and asked if any whites were about? The negro nearest us answered, "No, sah; massa was heah dis mornin', but he done gone home now." We then advanced to the fires, around which the negroes had collected to the number of ten or a dozen, large and small. Our wants were immediately made known to them. They were quite willing, even anxious to respond to our call for food. They offered to divide with us at noon, when "missus" brought their dinner out. We told them they would not have enough to spare, as there were six of us, and we were very hungry. The oldest negro or "boss hand," as he was called, then sent one of the younger ones to bring us something to eat. The negroes were all deeply interested in us, and were anxious to learn where our four comrades were hid. We told them, and inquired if that was a safe place. We were informed it was safe enough, but there was a better place south of it, across the ridge. We told the boss we would cross the ridge and look out a good hiding-place. He promised to bring our dinner to us as soon as it was brought to him where he was at work.

Sutherland and I then returned to our comrades and informed them it would not be long until we should have something to eat. In accordance with the advice received from our colored friends we gathered our things and moved across the ridge. We had passed the summit of the ridge and were going down its southern declivity when we came to a bench or level place, where we concluded to stop and make our bed. We had intended to go to the level ground near the base of the ridge, but on reaching the bench we knew of no reason why we should not stop there for the remainder of the day. We made our bed anew, and then washed our hands and faces, using the water from our bucket and canteen for that purpose. We then seated ourselves upon our bed, and quietly awaited the approach of the "boss" with our dinner. We had waited a short time, probably a half hour, when we saw him with a large bucket in hand near the base of the ridge hunting for us. One of our party rolled a small stone down hill toward him to let him know where we were. He soon discovered us, and climbed the hill-side, and delivered to us our dinner. We began eating immediately, and found we had been bountifully provided for. A bucket full of eatables, consisting of fried ham, fried eggs, boiled beans, and corn-dodgers, was furnished us. We had a keen relish for such fare, and devoured it all. When we had finished eating, the negro took his bucket and returned to his work; first telling us he would see us again in the evening. Our appetites were fully satisfied, and we covered ourselves in our bed and went to sleep.

We had slept but a short time before our rest was disturbed by a considerable noise. It was the noise of cavalry-men, without doubt, we thought, or of horses running at their utmost speed. We uncovered our heads and raised them slightly. On looking southward we saw two hounds pass near the base of the ridge. They ran swiftly, and were hot in pursuit of game. They were closely followed by three or four white citizens on horseback. The hounds and horsemen were soon out of hearing, and we felt greatly relieved. Just then the excitement of the chase was not agreeable to us. We were heartily glad we were not the objects of pursuit. Had we gone to the level ground, at the base of the ridge, before halting, as was at first intended, we would most likely have placed ourselves directly on the trail. The result to us in that case would have been unfortunate. As our hiding-place was on the steep side of the ridge, almost surrounded by small trees and brush, we thought it a safe one, and again gave ourselves over to rest. We slept well until late in the day. When we awoke the first object almost which met our vision was our colored benefactor sitting near us whittling a stick. He informed us we should have another meal at dusk. We told him any thing good to eat would be acceptable to us, and place us under lasting obligations to those who furnished it. We told him, too, that we had some Confederate money, and would buy as much provisions as he could deliver to us at dark, if it was not more than we could carry. He promised to see if we could be supplied, and told us to come up where they were at work after sunset.

As the day was already far spent, we began to fit up for another night's journey. On completing our preparations, we waited a few minutes longer for the sun to disappear in the west. Soon it had shed its last ray over us for the day, and we picked up our things and started from our retreat. By the twilight we made our way through the woods to the place where the negroes had been at work during the day. Just before dark we reached them. They had ceased from their labors and were expecting us. Some fruit pies fried in grease were furnished us for supper. While we were eating, the negroes asked what kind of provisions we could carry most of, or most conveniently. We told them we could do best on meat, salt, and meal. Two or three of them then went to bring us a supply of those articles. In due time they returned with a ham of meat, a little salt, half a bushel of meal, and half a dozen corn-dodgers. Wood had with him a clean pillow-slip, brought from the hospital. In it we put the corn-meal. The ham was cut in pieces and put in our haversacks. The salt was carried by one of our party in a blouse pocket.

On setting out we had the corn-dodgers, for which there was no room in our haversacks; and as, on account of their size, we could not get them into our blouse pockets without breaking them, we carried them in our hands until midnight. The ham had cost the negroes three dollars a pound, and it weighed twelve pounds and a half. We paid them thirty-seven dollars and fifty cents for it in Confederate shin-plaster. For the meal, salt, corn-bread, and what we had eaten during the day, we gave them twenty-two dollars and fifty cents. We paid them sixty dollars in all. It was not necessary, they did not exact it, but we had the scrip and were made no poorer by parting with it. It was current there at the time, and was much below par in the country we hoped to reach ere long.

We conversed briefly with the colored people before leaving them. We learned from them that we had traveled twenty-three miles the previous night, and that it was about forty miles to Rocky Mount Court-House, in Franklin county. It was growing late. The moon had risen, and was advancing in its 'course. Every hour of the night was precious to us and must be improved. We expressed to our benefactors our obligations. We thanked them heartily and sincerely. We told them they had no idea of the value of the service they had performed. It was a service to us; it was also a service to the cause in which we had struggled and suffered much. We could not pay them adequately, but hoped in the end they would have their reward in the results of the war.

We bade them good-night and left them, and sought the road immediately; on reaching it we could but contrast our feelings with those we had experienced on leaving it early in the morning. Our minds were at perfect ease on the question of supplies, as our pillow-slip was full, our haversacks were full, and each of us had a corn-dodger in his hand besides. We thought we should make a long stride toward our lines before our supplies should be exhausted. The meal in the pillow-slip was carried by turns. As we had eaten a great deal during the day we did not feel like walking rapidly. We put in the whole time, however, until after midnight, when we stopped to rest and eat some bread. A few minutes' rest sufficed, and we resumed our travels.

As no incident in our travels particularly interesting, or worthy of record, transpired for two or three nights or days, we pass on to the events of a subsequent date. We will say, first, that during the interval of time over which we pass without noting every circumstance of our journey, we were very cautious. In the night-time, while passing houses near the road, we maintained the strictest silence. We walked carefully, and even then the dogs often discovered us, and made the night dismal with their howling. We made it a rule not to allow daylight to find us upon the road; but before we go much farther in our narrative we will give an instance in which it did so find us. The first rays of the sun generally shone upon us in our bed asleep. During our waking hours in day-time, when hid in the lonely woods, we were careful not to talk, or laugh out boisterously, knowing the liability to be heard at a distance. We did not stand up or walk about a great deal. When we had supplies there was no occasion to incur risks, or purposely come in contact with any persons, black or white. We always hid, if possible, where water would be convenient to us. We had fire in day-time with which to broil our meat and make mush. During the day we prepared our midnight lunch. When we were in a secure retreat for the day we generally prepared a quantity of mush, for fear our hiding-place next day would be in a place too much exposed to admit of fire or smoke. In all our movements we tried to exercise the utmost caution. As the distance between us and our prison became greater we became, if possible, more cautious. The farther we got from prison the greater would be our disappointment in being caught and taken back.

The early morning of February 24th found us upon the road, which led through an open country. Cleared and fenceless lands bordered it on either side. We pushed on, in the hope of reaching woods, until broad daylight. At length the rays of the rising sun began to illuminate the face of Nature. We were then obliged to leave the public highway. The road had led us northward the last two nights, and still led us in that direction. We looked to our right, where the lands were hilly or a little broken. We went in that direction, thinking we could hide behind a knoll, or rising ground. Soon we gained a point or crest, from which the ground sloped gently to the east. A hundred yards or more ahead of us we saw the tops of scattering trees projecting above a bluff. We pressed on, and soon stood upon a precipice, and looked beyond it, over a narrow wooded valley. We clambered half-way down the precipice to hide among the rocks. We had laid our blankets, haversacks, and bag of meal aside. We were going to make our bed, but found the space in which we stood was not large enough for all of us. We would be hampered by the rocks. Smith and I had unrolled our blankets; Sutherland, Wood, Trippe, and Taylor had gone a little farther down among the rocks to find more room. About the same time we saw a smoke rising through the trees in the valley. We were sure a house was there, although we could not see it. It was south-east of us, apparently half a mile distant.

We were about beginning the preparations for our daily rest when the noise of an ax resounded in our ears. The noise was so unexpected and so near us that we were startled, and at first looked around wildly, and in amaze. We soon recovered from the shock of astonishment and surprise, and peered cautiously around the rocks and looked below us. Not more than a hundred yards from us, in the woods near the base of the precipice, we saw a single white man wielding his ax. His dog was near him. On account of the dog we lay low. If he had got a glimpse of us his master would have become aware of our presence. We could not make our bed; we could do nothing but keep still. Smith and I had near us all the blankets, and all the provisions belonging to our party. Our comrades were about thirty feet below us, almost under us. Smith ventured to drop their blankets to them, after which we all kept quiet. We slept but little. As long as the ax was used we felt no fear of being seen by the man, but every half hour we peered out from the rocks to see if the dog was near him.

About noon, or a little later, the man ceased chopping. We thought we should have a short respite while the man went to dinner, and would embrace that opportunity to eat our own. We looked out to see him leaving. We were greatly disappointed. A woman—his wife perhaps—had brought his dinner to him, and he was eating. She was accompanied by another dog. The two dogs then pranced and prowled about in the woods, and we watched them closely. We were fearful they would go around, and get above and behind us, but they did not do so. We were in a very restless and impatient mood; each moment seemed an hour almost. We would have parted with jewels, if we had possessed them, to have been away from there. When the man had finished eating, the woman took her bucket and went away, followed by the dogs. We were highly pleased to know the dogs were gone, for they had annoyed us greatly. The man resumed his toil unconscious of our presence. As he chopped almost incessantly, and could, therefore, look around but little, we felt a little safer. Smith and I opened our haversacks and took out some meat. We cut off a few thin slices and sprinkled them with meal. On raw meat and meal we made our dinner. While eating, Smith and I exhibited ourselves to our comrades below us. They looked up wishfully, and signified their desire to eat. As Smith and I had all the commissary stores we continued eating, to tantalize our comrades. At length we put some meal and a chunk of meat in a haversack and dropped it to them.

The day had been a long one to us. Our rest had not been refreshing. We were in constant apprehension and suspense. The loss of sleep and comfort, in consequence of having no bed, had its effect upon our bodies. We felt chilled and sore, and we longed for the approach of night. Near four o'clock, P. M., the wood chopper ceased from toil and went off with his ax on his shoulder. Erelong the sun went down, and, as soon as we got every thing ready, we climbed the precipice and went directly to the road. Early in the night we found we were about entering the suburbs of a town. It was Rocky Mount Court-House, Franklin county. We approached it on a road which bore a little west of north. We fell back a few paces and began our circuit around the place. On leaving the road we first climbed a fence and went across the corner of an inclosed tract of timber lands. We then climbed a second fence and entered open fields, in which we continued until the road north-west of the place was reached. In making our circuit we were guided by the lights in the town, which were yet burning. Near midnight we halted and eat some meal and meat, upon which, with an occasional swallow of water, we made a respectable supper.

On the morning of February 25th, as on the previous morning, we were in an open country. At daylight we looked ahead of us on the road, but saw no woods. A house, however, was discernible in the distance. As we dared not pass it, we left the road which had been leading us westward. South of the road, about half a mile, we saw a space of ground covered over with numerous rocks, large and small. To it we directed our steps, in the hope that the rocks would afford us shelter for the day. We soon reached the place, but did not much like it, and were loath to remain in its inadequate protection. But as the sun was up, we could not look for a better or more secure hiding-place without incurring even greater risks than there would be in making our bed, and keeping it during the day, where we were. We cleared the small rocks from a space sufficiently large for our bed and spread it upon the ground. We then lay down to sleep.

Our heads were near the base of a large rock which was between us and the road we had left a few moments before, and it hid us from view in that direction. To our right and left and at our feet were many rocks of smaller size, which partially concealed us as long as we lay low. On lying down we looked all around us, but scarcely a tree or bush was visible. Nothing but a waste of barren ground with an undulating and rocky surface could be seen. South of us, perhaps a little west, and nearly a mile distant, was higher ground. Beyond and above it, a few of the topmost branches of the tallest trees projected. The chief feature of the country immediately surrounding us was barrenness and nakedness. We could not resist the impression that our hiding-place was poorly chosen. A feeling of insecurity crept over us. The primeval forest of Virginia, with only the exception of the previous day, had hitherto protected us from the view of the rebellious citizens of the State. Near three hours of undisturbed repose was granted us.

Near ten o'clock, A. M., we were awakened by a clattering noise. Taylor looked out cautiously and discovered it was made by a wagon passing over a stony road. It was not on the road we had left in the morning, but on one just west of us, which crossed or intersected it. It was nearly two hundred yards from us. The man in the wagon was driving north-east, having come on the road from the south-west. On stopping in the morning we had not noticed the road, as the surface of the ground was a little broken, and many rocks and knolls intervened between it and ourselves. It had washed and worn considerably below the level of the ground. On finding we were so near a public highway, we felt uneasy, and still more dissatisfied with our hiding-place. We did not leave it yet, however, as the wagon had passed on out of hearing.

We again essayed to sleep. We fell into a kind of dozing sleep, from which we were soon aroused by the hum of voices. We looked westward and saw several persons, mostly women and children, walking on the road. They were a great while passing, it seemed to us, and were disposed to loiter by the way. We felt in an exceedingly disagreeable and unsafe position. At length the hum of voices died away and we tried to feel at ease, but could not. Very soon another rattling on the stony road disturbed our equanimity and patience. We looked and saw a cart on the road driven by a negro. It was a one-horse concern, and was followed by a white man on horseback. We judged we were not far from town, and resolved to flee our hiding-place, for fear some strollers, or home guards, or somebody should come upon us and report us, and take measures to recapture us.

We waited and watched until nearly noon, when, concluding there would be no passing on the road, we put our things in convenient shape for our first day-time traveling. Just as we had completed our preparations, we looked westward and northward to see if any persons were upon the road. We saw none. We immediately started southward, bearing slightly to our left. We did not run, but walked rapidly, without looking behind us. When we had gone about a mile, we reached a point from which we could look down an inclined plane into woods. We halted and looked all around us, but saw no one. We judged we had not been seen, and deemed our movement a successful one. We were glad to see woods once more, and pushed on until we stood in the midst of forest-trees.

We sat down on a large rock to rest and watch awhile. We were on a wooded hill-side, which sloped gently to the south-west. Trippe got up from his seat and went in a south-east course on the hill-side, to look for a place in which to hide. He was gone some time, and we became impatient for his return. We did not wish to leave the place where he had left us until he came back, as he would not know where to find us. Nearly a half hour passed before we saw Trippe returning. He was walking slowly and hesitatingly. He occasionally looked back in the direction he had gone. Before he reached us we discovered something wrong had happened; or if nothing wrong, something at least which we would rather had not transpired.

Trippe was vexed and almost spiritless. He had been recaptured once, and now he thought his time had come to be caught again and taken back to prison. He told us the cause of his discouragement. He had gone south-east of us, an eighth of a mile, or more, along the hill-side. He had turned directly south to go down hill, when he saw a man clad in "butternut" coming up hill. Trippe thought, and hoped, he had not been noticed by the citizen, and stood still to see if he would pass. The citizen came on up hill. His foot slipped, and he caught hold of a little tree to keep from falling. In getting around and above the tree his head turned slightly, and he noticed Trippe, about twenty steps from him. As soon as he recovered from his surprise he approached Trippe, and asked what he was doing there. Trippe said he was just looking through the woods a little. Other questions were asked, and answered by each party. Trippe tried at first to equivocate, but found it useless, as his uniform was plainly that of a Federal soldier. He told the citizen he had been a prisoner at Danville, and with others was trying to make his way to the Union lines. He also told him where we were, and how many there were of us in all. The citizen feigned sympathy with Trippe, and expressed a hope that he would get home all right. Trippe had very little faith in him. He advised Trippe not to fight any more against the South, and at the same time offered his hand. Trippe took the hand in his own with not the slightest confidence in its possessor. The Rebel pledged to Trippe his word and honor not to lay a straw in his path, and immediately turned and went directly back on his trail. Trippe watched him, and soon saw that he hurried himself, as if suddenly imbued with a new purpose.

When Trippe related the circumstance to us we became intent on getting away from there, as quickly and as far as possible. We placed no reliance in the promise of the Confederate not to lay a straw in our path, but thought he would take measures to interpose greater obstacles in the way of our progress. Our things being already in compact marching order, we started immediately. The meal in the pillow-slip, though not heavy, being more than two-thirds used, was all the surplus thing we had to carry. All else was in our haversacks. We went south-east, and soon reached the spot where the citizen had been encountered by Trippe. We then turned to our right and went south-west. On reaching the base of the ridge we found we would emerge from the woods and cross cleared lands, in a narrow valley, or change our course. There was no time for debate, and we pushed ahead.

Near the outskirts of the woods two little boys and a little girl were playing. As we passed, the largest boy cried out, "Uncle Jim has gone for the guards to catch you uns with." We hurried forward, scarcely taking time to thank the children for the information. If we had to be hunted we were glad to know it. A short distance ahead of us was a house. We passed near it, leaving it a little to our right. When we were just opposite the house, a woman came to the door and exhorted us to hurry. She said her brother-in-law was a "mean man," and had gone to report us to the home guards. As time was gold to us just then, we did not halt, but heeded the exhortation so earnestly given. As we crossed the branch which traversed the narrow valley we heard the woman say her husband had been killed in the war. She talked on, but we were soon out of hearing.

As we approached the upland, on the opposite side of the valley, we began to think about obscuring our trail. We noticed where a hollow, or ravine, entered the valley from the wooded hill-side. We got into the hollow and followed on its rocky bed, where we made no tracks, until we got some distance into the woods. A portion of the time we went on the double-quick, and sometimes, when on level ground or going down hill, we went even more rapidly. It was two o'clock, or a little later in the day, when we first halted to listen for "Uncle Jim" and his guards. We did not hear them, nor did we wish to; so we pressed on. We had so far traveled three miles or more, mostly in a western direction.

A point had been reached from which we could look across fields and open country in all directions, except south, southwest, and east—the course we should take in retracing our steps. As we did not wish to cross fields, or go back on our trail, we turned southward. In that direction we proceeded until we had gone over a mile, when we turned to our right, and again pushed rapidly westward, through a heavy wood. Soon we came to a branch of clear running water. As we were tired we concluded we would wade in the water, following the stream down, and thus obscure our trail. As we had made tracks in the wet soil near the branch on approaching it, we pushed on across it, going some distance until the solid ground was reached. We then got back to the branch, walking on scattering rocks, sticks, and logs, so as to leave no traces behind us. If the guards were on our trail, we hoped, when they reached the branch, they would cross it, and push on westward as speedily as possible.

We followed down stream in a south-west course for more than a mile. When in the water we traveled at a moderate gait, as the branch traversed a very narrow, thickly wooded valley, and we could not be seen at a distance. A point on the branch was at length reached where a road crossed it. The road had the appearance of being traveled a great deal, and we looked up and down it to see if any body could be seen. On seeing no one we crossed to the south of the road, still wading in the water. After getting a short distance into the woods, south of the road, we left the branch and pushed rapidly westward. Our feet had become wet, and we resorted to brisk walking to get our socks dry. We would have taken time to take our socks off and wring the water from them, but, should the guards come upon us, we did not wish to be barefooted.

Our flight was continued until sunset. We had intended traveling on a line parallel with the road, but found it necessary to bear southward occasionally to avoid crossing open fields. When the sun had gone down we called a halt. The country was very rough and broken where we halted; heavy woods and brushy undergrowth were all around us on all the hill-sides. We took refuge in a thicket, near a considerable bluff. No sounds of pursuers could be heard; every thing was still. We rested well, and slept a little. Our feet were worsted by the wetting they had received and our subsequent rapid walking. On a few scraps of meat dipped in meal we made a scanty supper. We dared not build a fire after dark or we would have made some mush and taken a fuller meal.

Before the moon arose it was very dark. We waited half an

hour or more for its appearance above the horizon. At length its light shone dimly through the woods. The sky was a little clouded and the woods were dense, but the moon served to guide us upon our course, if its light did shine imperfectly and at intervals. We gathered our things and started. We steered northward. When obliged to turn aside, or vary from that course, we varied to the west. Many difficulties beset us. Our hurried march in the day had considerably taxed our powers of endurance; our rest at dark was brief, only long enough for our limbs to stiffen; our feet were sore; we were hungry; our hasty meal at dark had not sufficed. It was the first we had eaten since midnight of the night before, on getting around Rocky Mount Court-House. The country was hilly; we got over and down one hill only to begin the ascent of another; the woods were dark, and logs and brush obstructed our pathway and impeded our progress. We persevered, however, and pressed on. One of our party went in advance and pushed the brush aside; the other five of us followed just behind him, in "close order."

Fully an hour passed before we emerged from the brush and woods into more open ground. We climbed a fence and crossed a field. On getting out of the field we struck a road running east and west. We followed it at a moderate gait until we had gone a mile, when we reached a cross-road. We then turned to our right and went due north. On going two miles or more we called a halt. We were much fatigued; nearly worn down, in fact, and, besides, we were faint and hungry. The road we were following seemed not to be much traveled. We had passed no house since dark. We had stopped on the road, where it was winding along the side of a ridge, which was heavily wooded. We determined to look for a retreat where we could rest awhile, build a fire, and make some mush. We left the road and went up hill west of it. Soon we gained the top of the hill or ridge. We then went down the hill on its western slope, and in the bushes near the foot of it we halted. The noise of rippling or running waters could be distinctly heard. Two of our party took our canteen and bucket and went to fill them. While they were gone we built a fire. A blanket was unrolled and spread on the bushes above the fire to partially conceal its light. Our bucket was then made three times full of mush. Small, thin slices and bits of meat were cut off and put in the mush as it was cooking. Soon our hunger was appeased, and our weariness hung not so heavily upon us. We put up our things, scattered our fire, sought the road, and resumed our journey.

Near midnight, and just after we had crossed a branch, we were startled by hearing a solitary shot in the woods. We immediately halted. Seemingly the sound of the shot came from a point not very far ahead of us, but some distance to our left. Our first conjecture was that we were in the vicinity of a cavalry bivouac. Two or three of our party thought the home guards had been posted on the roads, and were about to hem us in. There was no time to be lost in parleying, and we determined to go on slowly and slyly. Before going two hundred yards we came to a turn in the road. The road had been leading us northward, but on going around the turn it led us west. We again halted, thinking it was possible there was a guard on the road, as it led in the direction from whence the sound of the shot had proceeded. Trippe proposed going on a few paces to see. He did so. We followed him at the distance of fifty or sixty paces. In this way we advanced fully half a mile, when we reached a point where the road passed between fields. Trippe waited until we came up, when he pronounced the road clear, as far as pickets were concerned.

We then pushed on, and discovered we were about passing a house on the left of the road. We checked our speed and passed the house with care and celerity. When we had got about twenty steps beyond the house, and just as we were becoming careless again, the dogs began a lively barking. We proceeded a dozen steps further when we noticed the sparks of a fire flying upward. The fire was about twenty steps ahead of us, on the left of the road. It was near the corner of the rail-fence, where the lane terminated. We stopped instantly, but said nothing. We watched the fire closely for a moment. The dogs kept up their howling. In the light of the fire, which soon blazed up, we distinctly saw several covered wagons ahead of us near the road side. We knew, or thought at least, that we were about running into a supply train. We hardly knew what to do. The dogs continued barking furiously, and would soon arouse somebody, to see what disturbed them. We could not go forward, as the guards, or teamsters, with the train would discover us. We did not wish to go back by the house, as there was danger of being observed by persons within, or about it. There was no time for deliberation. We climbed the rail-fence to our right on the north of the road. We were careful not to make any noise; although the dogs made hubbub enough to drown any noise we should make.

We had left tracks on the road, and found on getting into the field that its surface was moist and impressible. We determined to make a trail that would mislead any person who might have the curiosity to follow us. On reaching a point in the field about a quarter of a mile due north of the road we turned east. In that direction we traveled half a mile. We then turned south and crossed the fence at the corner of the field. On getting into the road we followed it east nearly a quarter of a mile, when we went some distance in a south-east course. By so doing we got into thick woods where the ground was covered with leaves, where we could leave only very indistinct traces behind us. We then turned and traveled directly west, keeping parallel with the road, and a little more than a quarter of a mile south of it. The dogs at the house still kept up their howling; and as the train and those with it were just at hand, we kept off at a safe distance. The shot we had heard an hour before, we judged had been fired by some one with the train.

When we had gone far enough, in a western direction, to reach a point directly south of the house, where the dogs were still barking, we bore considerably to our right, and went north-west. We continued in that direction until we struck the road some distance west of the wagon train. After going something more than a mile further on the road, in a direction a little north of west, we halted. It lacked an hour or more of being daylight, but as we were very tired, having traveled many miles in the last twenty-four hours, we determined to look out for a secure hiding-place for the day. We accordingly left the road and penetrated some distance into the woods on the north of it. Just after crossing a small branch we halted, and made our preparations for a refreshing sleep. We fell into a sound slumber immediately on lying down on our bed.

About mid-day we awoke and found ourselves very stiff and sore all over. We felt very little like moving about. We had pulled off our shoes on lying down, and on getting up we found our feet were so very sore that we could hardly get them on again. The sky was overcast with clouds, threatening snow. Our stock of provisions was getting very low, and other circumstances seemed to conspire in making the woods around us and the prospect before us quite cheerless. That we had not fallen into the hands of the home guards was the only circumstance that afforded us consolation. After getting our shoes on, we set about building a fire. We went to the branch near us and washed our hands and faces; afterward feeling some better. Our vessels were filled with water at the branch, to be used in making mush. When we had dispatched our dinner we had some meal left, also a little salt, but no meat. The meal was emptied from the pillow-slip and made into mush, which, with the exception of the last bucket full made, was put into the pillow-slip. The last mush made was left in the bucket. When the mush became cold it sliced off nicely, and was ready for our midnight meal.

Shortly after noon one of our party wandered out northward from our hiding-place some distance, and spied a man engaged in plowing in an old field. It was early in the season, we thought, for plowing, but as we had seen plowing near Danville in January, we knew it was nothing unusual for that country. Sutherland and I went out and lay close to the fence which inclosed the field, to watch the man who was plowing, and see if we could determine whether he was white or black. It so happened that he did not plow on out to the fence near which we were hid, as a strip of sod or grass land intervened between him and the fence. We were somewhat disappointed, as we could not make out at that distance whether the man was white or black. If we had been assured he was a black man, we would have made an effort to procure more food.

Near the close of the day we went to the branch and bathed our feet thoroughly, hoping, if it did not improve them, it would keep them from getting sorer than they were already. We then lay down and slept about an hour, and on waking we found that our blankets and the ground were covered with snow to the depth of an inch. We got up and shook the snow from our blankets, and put every thing in order for the night's marching. Awhile before sunset the snow ceased falling, the clouds began to clear away, and the weather was perceptibly cooler. No clouds obscured the sun as it shed its last rays over us for the day, and sank from view in the west.

Just at dark we left our hiding-place and went directly to the road. It was quite dark, as the moon had not appeared; but as our feet were sore, we could only advance slowly any how, and we pushed on. In the road, where there were no leaves, the snow had melted, making the walking slippery and slavish. When the moon arose we walked at the side of the road, and got along some better. Early in the night Taylor began to fall behind. Sore feet, we judged, was the cause of his slow progress. He fell behind several times, and we waited as often for him to come up. We asked him no questions, only supposing that his feet were sorer than our own. About ten o'clock, or a little later in the night, we struck a pike running north-east and south-west. The road we had been following did not cross it. As we had to change our course, and as Taylor was some distance behind, we waited for him to catch up. When he had caught up we waited awhile longer for him to rest.

On renewing our travels we followed the pike in a north-east course toward Lynchburg. Before going very far on the pike, we passed one house on the left. We went nearly half a mile beyond the house, when we discovered an obscure road leading westward. We changed our course, as we wished to reach and cross the Blue Ridge Mountains as soon as possible. Taylor had kept up with us while following the pike, but again fell behind on leaving it. The road was a poor one. Its clay surface had been considerably moistened by the melting snow, late in the day and early in the night. Before midnight the mud began freezing, and it stuck tenaciously to our shoes. The country was rough and broken, and the road led us over a succession of ridges and hollows. In breaking the frozen crust of mud our feet were continually slipping backward or forward, or sideways, as we went up and down the hills, making our march extremely fatiguing and wearisome. We were obliged to keep the road on account of the trees, logs, and brush near it on either side. Our way, however, was plain before us, as the road looked black in contrast with the snowy woods.

We trudged on in the difficult and lonely way, and, though our progress was slow, Taylor had fallen far behind. Near midnight we were on the point of stopping to eat some mush, but concluded to move on slowly for awhile, and give Taylor a chance to catch up with us or gain on us. We slackened our pace considerably, and, on going half a mile, we halted at the road side. Taylor had not caught up with us, neither was he in sight or hearing. We sat on a log, and waited patiently for his approach. Several minutes passed while we were waiting. We took the mush from our bucket and cut it in slices ready for eating. While so doing Taylor came dragging himself along the road. We called to him, and he turned aside to join us in the woods. He was lame and weary. On reaching us he sank almost exhausted to the ground, sitting in the snow and placing his back against the log upon which we sat. We made no inquiries of Taylor as to the cause of his lameness, supposing he could not tell us more than we knew already.

One or two observations were made respecting the bad condition of the road, after which we began eating our midnight lunch. When we had finished eating we gathered our things and started. Trippe and I were ahead, and had reached the road and gone on it a few steps. Wood and Sutherland were closely following us. Sutherland looked back and saw Smith coming, but did not see Taylor. Sutherland then asked, "Smith, where is Taylor? an't he coming?" Smith answered, "I thought he was following me;" and then looked behind and called aloud, "Come on, Taylor." Smith not understanding Taylor's reply, went back to him. On being asked why he had not started, Taylor said he was unable to go any farther, as his broken leg had failed him. Smith at once called to us to come back to the place where Taylor was. We did so. It was painfully apparent that he could go no farther that night. We learned for the first time that he had been wounded in the leg, and had one of its bones broken. He was not a Chickamauga prisoner, but had been wounded and captured at or near Leesburg, Virginia, in a cavalry engagement, early in July, 1863, at the time of the battles of Gettysburg, Pennsylvania. During our four or five weeks' association with him it so happened we had not learned of his wound.

We at once concluded that our travels for that night were at an end, and began looking around for a place in which to lie over until the following night. When Taylor heard our determination he objected, saying he felt sure he would not be able to travel by the following night, and might not be able to renew the journey for a week. He would not consent that we should remain with him until the next night, unless he knew he would be able to go on with us by that time. We insisted on waiting with him as long as that, as we should lose only three hours' time by so doing. Taylor still objected, saying he would not detain us a single hour, and if we failed in reaching the lines, it should not be laid to his charge. We determined to remain, when Taylor assured us he could not travel for at least three or four nights, and was unwilling to feel himself responsible for the consequences that might ensue from so long a detention of our party. We then offered to divide our party, to leave two with Taylor, and let the other three go on. But he objected to this proposal also, saying he would not delay a single one of us, and probably be the cause, immediate or remote, of the return of that one to prison. He would rather take his chances of ultimately reaching the lines alone, and feel clear of responsibility for any accident or disaster that might overtake us than to do otherwise.

We had offered fairly, as we thought, and concluding Taylor

"Left Alone."—Page 53.

knew the nature and extent of his disability much better than we did, we determined to leave the case to him. If he said remain, we would cheerfully do so; or if he said for us to go on and leave him behind, we would do that regretfully. Taylor then said for us to lose no time on his account, but to push on to the Union lines, and make our escape good. It required but a few moments to arrange for resuming our journey, and to advise Taylor as to the best course to pursue; to say to him the parting good-by, and leave him behind. The mush in the pillow-slip, all the provisions we had, except a little salt, was then taken out and divided into six parts. The largest part was given to Taylor. The other five parts were put in our haversacks. Nearly or quite half of the scrip on hand was given him, as he was going to tarry awhile in the Confederacy, and might use it to advantage. A portion of the salt was also given him. The canteen which had been used by our party so far on the trip, and which belonged to Taylor, was left with him. He had a watch and a supply of scrip to barter for food, or for the services of a guide, to conduct him to the lines, or both. With these, and with his canteen and haversack, we left him alone in the woods, wrapped in his overcoat and blanket. It was a sad and melancholy scene we witnessed in parting from Taylor. It was painful and trying to us to shake his hand, and say to him "good-by." Our feelings were similar to those occasioned by the fall of a comrade on the battle-field. We had left Taylor, and were getting into the road when we heard him say, "Company G, 2d Massachusetts Cavalry," giving his address, and asking us to write to him if we reached the lines. We each of us then gave him the name of the company and regiment to which we respectively belonged, so that he might write to us if he got through all right.

The substance of the advice we gave to Taylor was to remain where he was until daylight, at which time he could move to a better or more secure hiding-place, if able to do so, where he could command a view of the road, and see persons that might pass upon it. The first negro, or party of negroes, he saw passing, if no whites were with them, he was to hail, and beckon them to him and make his condition known, and get them to harbor him, or take him to some house where he could be harbored until he was able to renew his journey. If he saw no person pass during the day, he was to go in the evening in search of a habitation where assistance might be given him. When able to travel, he was to secure, if possible, the services of a guide, to conduct him to some point within or in the vicinity of the pickets or outposts of our army. He could reward his guide, if fortunate enough to secure one, with his watch and Confederate money.

It was the night of Friday, February 26, 1864, that we left Taylor behind. We left him within six miles of the Blue Ridge Mountain, at a point between eighty and one hundred miles south-west of Lynchburg, Va., and nearly three miles west of the pike leading to that place. We must have left him somewhere near the boundary line between Franklin and Bedford counties, Va., in the north-west corner of one, or in the south-east corner of the other. If it was trying to us to part with Taylor and leave him, it must have put his resolution and self-denial to a severe test to persist in being left alone in his crippled and almost helpless condition. On stopping he was warm, as the road was bad, and he had exerted himself to catch up with us. By sitting down in the snow, he cooled suddenly, and his lame leg became stiff and useless. His condition was critical and unenviable, as he was unable to move about with ease or comfort, and his supply of food was small in quantity and poor in quality. No house was near him. We had not passed a house since leaving the pike. The weather was cold, as the snow and mud was freezing. He was in a bleak mountain country alone. No friend was near him. We had been his friends and comrades, and were his friends still, but had forsaken him. His prospect was cheerless. His desponding heart had little on which to predicate a hope. He dreaded to meet a man of his own color, for fear of meeting an enemy, and in the mountain districts the blacks were few. The woods around him were dreary, although the ground was covered with snow, and the moon shone brightly. The trees with their leafless branches and skeleton shadows could be dimly seen, but were poor companions for a maimed and wearied traveler in an enemy's land. It was a touching, but a necessary or unavoidable incident of our journey to leave Taylor behind in the Winter, and in the wilderness, as a lonely and solitary sentinel in the silent watches of the night. But we could do no better, as our supply of provisions was nearly exhausted, and we could not recruit it, or seek assistance for him without jeopardizing his safety as well as our own. So we left him to whatever fate might fall to him in the merciful dispensation of Providence.

I have never heard from or of Taylor to this date, December, 1869. Whether he got able to travel, and succeeded in making his escape from the Confederacy, or whether he was recaptured and returned to prison, is not known to me. He may have perished from starvation where we left him, on account of inability to get away from there.

CHAPTER III.

PROVISIONS GONE—CROSS THE BLUE RIDGE—SECURING FOOD—GOING THROUGH BIG LICK—RAIN AND DARKNESS—WE ARE COMPELLED TO SEEK SHELTER—LYING OVER—THE TOBACCO—ITS OWNER—MORE FOOD LAID IN—UP THE VALLEY—STRIKE FOR THE ALLEGHANIES—DIFFICULT TRAVELING—ROUGH COUNTRY—WE REACH A STREAM—TOO WEARY TO FORD—FALL BACK TO HIDE—MAKING OUR BED—FALL ASLEEP.

HAVING parted with Taylor, our travels were resumed through the later hours of the night. Once or twice in traveling the distance of four, or four and a half miles, we almost concluded to return to him, but feared disaster might come upon us if we turned back. It soon became evident that daybreak was at hand, but we proceeded a mile farther before turning into the woods. The sun was just rising when we began making our bed, for the 27th of February, in a place surrounded by woods and brush. On lying down we fell asleep. We awoke about the middle of the afternoon. Shortly after arousing from our slumbers, we eat the last of our mush. A little salt was all re had left of the supplies we had received from our negro friends in Henry county. When, where, and how our next supply of food should be secured we did not know. We judged we should cross the mountain during the approaching night, and determined to give ourselves no concern on the score of rations until the valley on the other side was reached.

The sad event of the previous night formed the subject of our conversation for the evening. "It would n't surprise me a bit," said Wood, "if Taylor should beat us to the lines yet."

"He may," said Trippe, "if he lives through the first night or two, does well, and is lucky enough to secure the services of a good guide to take him through by the short cuts."

"Our lines will be down this way some of these days," said Smith.

"The only difficulty with Taylor," remarked Trippe, "will be in avoiding Rebel citizens and finding a true Union friend to care for him a few days."

"He must have nothing to do with any body but a negro," said Sutherland, "or he's a goner." "Boys," he continued, "supposing it should become necessary for us to separate into two squads, how 'll we divide?"

"Draw cuts," answered Wood.

"If it should become necessary for us to separate," remarked Trippe, "it will most likely be under such circumstances as will forbid drawing cuts."

"Yes, boys," answered Wood, "we 'll have to draw cuts now, and have the thing understood."

Five small sticks were accordingly prepared. They were of two different lengths. It being understood how the division should stand, we drew cuts. It was decided that Smith, Wood, and Sutherland should go in one direction, while Trippe and I should go in another. We determined, however, never to separate unless no other alternative would answer, and to push on and endeavor to reach our lines together.

At sunset we began arranging our things for journeying. As soon as it was dark we sought the road, and on reaching it we heard voices. We retired a few paces into the bushes and waited until a half dozen or more persons, mostly if not all colored, had passed by. "Now, boys," whispered Wood, as the women and children were passing, " here is a good chance to get something to eat." But we had decided to cross the mountains before looking after food, and allowed the opportunity to pass. We then set out on our ninth night of travel, and had gone but little more than a mile when we came to a considerable branch. We crossed it with but little trouble, and soon after passed near a house on the road whose occupants had not retired for the night. We got by the house without attracting attention, or at least without exciting curiosity. On following the road a little further, we found it commenced its winding ascent of the mountain, passing through a gap near the boundary line between Franklin and Bedford counties, Va. We had heard before leaving prison that the Blue Ridge Mountains were infested with bush-whackers. We had a wholesome dread of these, and advanced cautiously up the road, hoping, if there were any, we should hear or see them before they should hear or see us.

In little more than an hour's time we reached the highest point in the gap, over which the road passed. We met with no one to dispute our progress, and the descent of the western slope was immediately commenced. We had followed the road but a short distance down the mountain-side, when, on making a turn in the road, we saw a light ahead, apparently about one hundred yards distant from us. Judging it to be the light of a torch, or small fire, we halted, and, on doing so, we heard voices engaged in conversation. Trippe at once proposed going ahead alone a few yards to see what might be seen. We consented, and he did so. A few minutes of intense anxiety to us passed, as we imagined the reports concerning bush-whackers were about to be verified. Before Trippe returned we heard a door shut, the fire or light at the same time disappearing. We then knew there was a house, or hut of some kind, near the road, not far from us; but of the number and character of its occupants we were not so well informed. .

On coming back to us Trippe reported a house down there, and the light we had seen was the light of a fire in the house.

Trippe said, further, that some one was just leaving the house, and, as soon as that person had started off down the road, the conversation ceased, and the door of the house was closed. We waited a few minutes for the folks in the house to get to sleep, and for the person on the road ahead of us to get out of our way, when we again started forward. On coming to the house we found it a very small one, situated within a few steps of the road. Passing it without discovery, we slowly walked on, and in due time reached the valley below.

Near the foot or base of the ridge was what appeared to be a considerable stream of water; but on reaching it we found it to be more wide than deep. We went a short distance down stream and found four foot logs, from sixteen to twenty feet long, extending across the stream. On these we crossed, and on reaching the opposite side we halted for awhile to rest before proceeding to the road.

"If we only had some meat and bread," said Smith, "now would be a good time to eat it."

"This would be a good place, too," added Sutherland, "as water is handy."

"I guess we would n't be particular as to the place," observed Smith, "if we only had something to eat."

Being reminded of the fact that we were out of rations we resolved to try our luck at the first house that came in our way. We were not long in reaching one, probably not more than half an hour. As we had crossed the mountain without difficulty; as we felt glad we had not met with guerrillas—felt considerably hungry, and were, withal, much emboldened, we were not overcautious in our movements. Each of our party of five entered the yard through the gate in front, and on reaching the house—an old two-story frame house, unpainted—we rapped violently at the front door. There was no answer from within. We called and rapped repeatedly, but with the same results. We then passed around the house to its south side, where we found another door. Sutherland knocked loudly on it, but no response came. He then put his mouth to the string-hole and asked, "Is any body at home?"

A man inside answered, in a tone of voice indicating fright, "I guess there's somebody about."

"Why don't you get up, then?" asked Sutherland. "Nobody's going to hurt you."

"What do you want?" inquired the man.

"We want something to eat, and want you to get up and set about getting it forthwith," said Sutherland. He refused to even get out of bed, whereupon Sutherland demanded, "Shall we burst your door down?" and Wood added, "and come in and burst your noggin?"

The man said, "That rests with you," and inquired, "Who are you, and where are you going?"

"We are soldiers going to Rocky Mount Court-House," Sutherland answered.

"Go on over the mountain, and you will be fed in the morning," returned the man.

Preferring to risk our chances at the next house to doing any very rash or violent acts, we left this one, telling the man he showed a very poor quality of patriotism.

"If it was any other time, if it twas daylight, I might do something for you."

"We don't have to stand picket in the night-time; we don't have to march, skirmish, and frequently fight in the night-time, I suppose?" retorted Sutherland, in a very unamiable voice.

"And skedaddle in the night-time from such rusty Butternuts as you are," added Smith, in a tone just loud enough not to be heard by the man, as we were withdrawing from the yard.

We passed out of the yard through the gate to the road as quickly as we could, intending to hurry on our way. As Sutherland closed the gate he threatened the man with, "We shall report you when we get to Rocky Mount, mark that."

On starting forward on the road Wood observed, "We commenced too heavy on the gentleman: we got him so badly scared he didn't know what to do, or how to do it."

We kept up our conversation, dwelling chiefly on the causes, real and supposed, of our failure in procuring food, and of the method to be resorted to in supplying our necessities. It was agreed that Wood and I should try our hands at the next house. It was after midnight, and should we not reach the next house soon we decided not to disturb its inmates, as we must have time to get out of reach after so doing before hiding for the day.

In a few moments we halted in front of a house on the south of the road at a distance of sixty or seventy yards from it. Wood and I entered the yard and approached a door in the one-story part of the house, supposing the darkies slept there. On knocking slightly at the door, and hearing no answer, we jerked the latch string once or twice. A voice inside—which was undoubtedly that of an elderly white person—remonstrated strongly against being disturbed at so late an hour. Wood seeing the smoke-house a few steps to his left, went to examine it, and proceeded from thence to the yard south of the house.

At the same time I stepped upon the porch in front of the two-story part of the house, and walked on it until I discovered a pair of steps or stairs. On going up the steps I found the porch had a second story also. Just at the top of the steps was a doorway to the second story of the main building. I found the door fastened, when I called out, asking if any one was inside. A voice, plainly that of a negro, answered there was. I told him to get up, and come out doors, as there were some folks at the road who would like very much to see him. The negro declined, saying, "You can't come dat game on dis chile: se not coming out dar."

"Get out of bed and come to the string hole," said I, "I want to speak to you." He did so, when I said, "Put your ear to the string-hole." He complied; and in a loud, distinct whisper, I pronounced the word "Yankees." As soon as the negro could draw on his clothing, the bar of the door came down and he and I descended the steps into the yard.

On seeing us, Wood approached, saying to the negro, "Where did you come from?"

"Ise from Knoxville," was the answer.

"But just now, where did you come from just now?" asked Wood.

"From up in the loft," was the negro's reply.

"Come out to the road, old fellow," said I, "there's some more Yankees out there."

"Lord, massa! golly! dat so?" ejaculated the astonished negro.

We then went to the road accompanied by the negro. On rejoining Trippe, Smith, and Sutherland, at the point where we had left them, the last named, on seeing the negro, remarked, "You don't expect us to eat that fellow, do you?"

We lost no time in telling the negro what was wanting; that we were hungry and had no provisions. The negro said the cellar and smoke-house were locked, and the old master had the keys. We asked him how soon he could get something for us to eat. He replied, "In the mornin', 'fore massa and mistress gits up."

"How about the keys; don't the whites get up and unlock?"

"No, sah; we gits de keys, onfastens, and gits breakfast 'fore de white folks gits out o' bed," replied the negro.

On ascertaining beyond doubt that provisions would be furnished us in the morning, we had the negro conduct us to a safe hiding-place for the day, which was near at hand. He took us to a secure retreat in the midst of a large grove of heavy oak timber situated about a mile from the house, on the north of the road. In all directions from our hiding-place for the day—Sunday, February 28th—were open fields. The woods or grove we were in covered three or four hundred acres of land. Our camp for the day was close to a rivulet, and was immediately surrounded by tall dead grass; and a little further from us were numerous small trees and bushes. The negro told us he would fetch us breakfast by ten o'clock, and then hurried home.

It was an hour or more before day when we made our usual preparations for sleep. Soon after lying down we were lost in slumber. Near nine o'clock, A. M., we awoke from our slumbers and got up and washed our faces at the rivulet. Our toilet completed, we had not long to wait for the appearance of our negro friend, with a small basket of eatables, a pitcher of milk, and a mug of molasses. We fared sumptuously on wheat cakes, fried bacon, potatoes, molasses, and milk. When we had finished our meal the negro took the molasses and milk pitchers in his basket and went homeward. While eating we learned from the negro that we were in Roanoke county, and that the nearest town on the road we expected to travel was Big Lick, a station on the East Tennessee and Virginia Railroad.

Shortly after noon the negro came out and talked quite a while with us. He wished to know when we would have another meal brought out. We expressed our willingness to receive another meal at any time before sunset. We asked the negro how much provision he could furnish us to carry with us. He replied that he had not a good chance in day-time to get at the meat, flour, and potatoes, without being seen by his master or mistress, and at night he had no chance at all to secure any thing, as the cellar and smoke-house were always locked at dark by the whites, who kept the keys until morning.

The man on whose provision we were subsisting was named Schooler, or Schuyler. Being an original secessionist, he left Knoxville, Tennessee, and settled in Roanoke county, Virginia, where he would be less troubled with Federal troops. The negro had also lived in Knoxville, and had before seen Yankee soldiers. When he left us he went home, and soon returned with another supply of food for our present consumption. While we were eating, the negro informed us that Schooler, his master, had seen the man at whose house we had attempted to get rations on the previous night. The man told Schooler of the demonstrations we had made at his house before leaving it to go on over the mountain. Schooler in turn told the man that he, too, had been interrupted during the night, but the disturbers of his sleep had done no harm, and gone on, he knew not where.

Our supper finished, we had an understanding with the negro as to the place where we should receive the corn and meat. He then left us, and we rolled up our blankets and made other needful preparations for our tenth night's travel. Just at dark we started for the point designated to receive what provisions our negro host could provide for us. As we found him there with the corn and meat, we were not long delayed. We were told it was seven miles to Big Lick, and that Salem Court-House was nine miles west of that place. I gave the negro one of my blouses as a slight compensation for his services to us, and as a token of remembrance. We thanked the negro heartily for befriending us in the hour of need, and then put the corn, which was shelled, in our haversacks, and the meat in our pillow-slip, and started for the road, accompanied that far by the negro.

On reaching the road we bade our negro friend farewell and left him. We found the road better than we expected, and pushed forward rapidly, hoping to get around Big Lick by midnight. We had thought of bearing to our right and passing east of the place. As soon as we thought we had gone six miles we saw a few small houses not far ahead of us, and concluded to pass them before commencing our circuit around the town. When we were just opposite the first house, Wood supposed it to be the domicile of a negro family, and went to the door, opened it, and asked how far it was to Big Lick. "You are there now," was the answer given. Closing the door without asking any more questions, Wood hastily rejoined us at the road.

On finding we were in town we pushed on through it, walking silently and briskly. Near the railroad depot we halted, and after consulting briefly concluded to leave the road, so as to elude pursuers, fearing the man we had inquired of might be a white Rebel, and might collect a party to look after us in the morning. After leaving the road we reached in a few minutes' time the railroad bridge. We passed under the bridge, walking partly in the waters of the little stream which it spanned until we gained the woods north of the railroad. We then traveled due northward until the sky became cloudy, when it grew much darker, and we found great difficulty in making our way through strange woods, with no road to guide us.

Before morning it began raining, and the night became black and dismal in its last hours. We could scarcely proceed, but we kept on the move. Just at daylight we came to a road running east and west. It seemed to be a very public one. As it was raining hard we thought we should not be seen, and we crossed the road and pushed on northward something more than a mile, when we halted in the midst of a considerable forest of pines. Through this forest was a string of rail-fence, and as it was raining hard, so that we could not make our bed down on the ground, we placed rails across from one panel to another, on which we sat with our coats and blankets disposed about us so as to shed the water off as much as possible. In this manner we occupied two corners of the fence; three of us in one corner and two in the other.

Near noon we were compelled by the severity of the storm to seek shelter. We started and kept close to the fence on its north side, going in an easterly direction. In a few minutes we came to another fence, running north through open fields. We changed our course, and followed it until we came to a branch running in a south-east course. As the ground was much lower near the branch we could follow it and at the same time be screened from view. Soon we came in sight of a lone building to our left a short distance, in the edge of the woods. We went directly to it, and found it to be a tobacco-house. In it we found shelter from the rain, as the roof was good. We then took off our coats and blankets, and wrung the water from them. As there was a lot of corn-blades tied in bundles stacked in one corner of the room, we soon had a good resting-place. A small lot of tobacco leaves, hanging above our heads, soon attracted our attention, when the following conversation took place:

"There's some tobacco," said Smith. "I'll bet there will be somebody out here before night to look at it."

"Not while it rains this way," said Trippe.

"Well, let them come," said Wood, "it belongs to nobody but a darkie, any how."

"And when he comes out here we'll only have him to furnish us with more rations," said Sutherland.

"I'm only afraid he won't come," added Trippe.

There was no floor in the tobacco-house, and we cleared the corn-blades and straw from the center and built a fire. For fuel we used tobacco sticks, of which there was a large quantity piled up in a corner of the building. After burning enough sticks to make sufficient coals and ashes for the purpose, we went to parching corn. This we did by scattering the corn near the fire and raking hot ashes and coals over it. When the corn was parched sufficiently, we raked it from the ashes with small sticks. After eating all we wished of parched corn and broiled meat, we parched a lot of corn for future use.

The rain continued falling, and the day was far spent, when we came to the conclusion we should be compelled to lie over for the approaching night—February 29th. At dark we stretched our blankets on sticks around the fire, for the twofold purpose of drying them and concealing the fire. Soon we were obliged to allow the fire to go down, as its light shone against the roof and through the cracks of the building between the logs. We had seen but one house during the evening from where we were, and that was away some distance to the north of us. But for fear somebody would be passing, and see the light of our fire, and thus discover us, and publish the fact of our presence in the vicinity, we put it out entirely. Becoming reconciled to the necessity of stopping over for the night and following day, we thought we would make the best of it, and rest, and recuperate as much as possible in that time. So, taking time and pains, and a goodly quantity of corn-blades, we made us a good bed. A roof over our heads and the pelting rain-storm without were conducive to sleep, and the night was passed in quiet and repose.

We waked up shortly after daylight in the morning, but did not get out of bed until about eight o'clock, A. M. The rain had ceased, but clouds still overspread the sky, causing us to feel doubtful about getting off even that night. We went out one at a time to the pools of water, and washed our hands and faces. Soon after we built a fire and began parching corn, and broiling meat for breakfast and dinner. While thus engaged, Sutherland, looking through a crack between logs, espied an old negro approaching. As he was alone he gave us no concern, and we were not averse to his coming. Approaching nearer and nearer the building, the old negro finally came upon our trail and noticed our tracks. He followed them a few steps, when, discovering they led to the tobacco-house, he came to a halt. He watched the house closely for a moment or two, when hearing or seeing us, he turned to go back. Sutherland opened the door and said, "Hullo, old man! that 'll never do; come in here, we 'll not hurt you."

The old man turned about, and after further entreaty approached the house and entered it. He had come out to examine his tobacco. He was well stricken in years, being ninety years of age, having children, grandchildren, and great grandchildren. On account of his age he was slow of speech and comprehension. We had trouble in getting him to understand who and what we were, and the situation in which we were placed. He did not seem, at first, to correctly understand the meaning of the term Yankee, but soon came to it, inquiring, "Is you uns some of them fellers that 's penned up in the 'backer-houses in Richmond?" We answered that we were. We found it necessary to impress on his mind the necessity of keeping secret from the whites the fact of our presence in the country. Our need of procuring provisions from time to time was also explained to the old man. We urged the old man to either bring or send us some meat of some kind, if nothing else, and to have it at the tobacco-house by sunset. He promised to do so, and shortly after examining and arranging his tobacco, he went slowly on his way home. We finished our breakfast, and continued parching corn for awhile. A little before noon we laid-ourselves down, and slept until about three o'clock in the evening.

On getting up we finished parching corn, and then all the provisions we had with us were ready for eating. When we first got up the sky was partially clear, and by sunset it was cloudless. Just after sunset the old negro arrived with some six or eight pounds of meat, mostly boiled beef, the remainder being a small piece of side meat. A couple of corn-dodgers were also furnished us, which we set apart for our midnight meal. Having got our baggage, quartermaster and commissary stores, ready for the trip, we expressed our obligations to the aged negro who had befriended us, and bade him good-by. He then started home, and soon after we set out on our eleventh night's journey, March 1, 1864.

Finding the ground soft and well saturated with water, we

thought we should do well if we trudged through eight or ten miles that night. On reaching the road, which had been pointed out to us by the negro, we found the walking much better than we expected, as the water could not so easily penetrate its hard surface. In a short time we passed the house where lived the owner of the plantation to which the tobacco-house in which we had been sheltering belonged. The house was near the road, and the lights in it were burning brightly. While we were passing the house the dogs began a lively barking, and kept it up until we had gone some distance, and crossed a creek, when we heard no more of them. Near midnight we halted at the road side amid a cluster of small trees, and eat some beef and corn-bread.

We soon resumed our travels. As we could not walk very rapidly, owing to the condition of the road, we put in the whole time until day-break, so that we could have it to say that we were at least eight or ten miles nearer our goal than when setting out. The road we were traveling bore northward in its general direction, but as the country on either side was covered with unfenced woods, it frequently deviated from its general course. At length day-break came, and we went to the left of the road in search of a secure hiding-place for the day, March 2, 1864.

The distance gone over during the night had not been more than eleven miles, or twelve at the furthest, but we were that distance further north, which was a gratifying feature of the night's journey. The ground being yet very damp, we were compelled to seek an open space in which to make our bed, and a quantity of brush and leaves on which to make it, so that our bedding should not get damp or muddy. A suitable hiding-place having been found, we collected leaves and brush from the adjacent woods, and made our bed on them, and retired to sleep for the day. We went about a mile from the road before locating our camp. It was further than may have been necessary, as the road was not a very public one, judging from appearances, and the country was very sparsely settled.

Some time in the evening we awoke and got up, finding the

sky clear, and the weather mild for the time of year. We found we had not stopped convenient to water, but on looking around a little we found water not far off sufficient for our needs. As we had no use for fire we built none, but made a meal on parched corn and beef, and quietly awaited the approach of night. The evening was spent in conversation, dwelling chiefly on our trip, past and prospective. We talked of things that had taken place, which, if we had them to do over again, we should do differently; of some fork of the road or cross-road, where, if we were only there again, we would take a different course. Sometimes we would imagine certain things to happen us, and decide in our minds what we should do, should the event actually transpire. Our minds seemed always occupied, either with thoughts and reflections on the journey, so far as completed, or with plans and expedients for the journey yet before us.

At dark our luggage was fitted up in readiness for starting out on the twelfth night of our travels, being the thirteenth night out. In a half hour's time we were on the road, wending our way northward. We found the road had improved under the day's sunshine, and we were enabled to make better progress than we had made on the previous night. On coming to a cross-road near midnight we stopped a few minutes to eat a little and consult as to the course to take, north or west. It was evident that, no matter which course we took, we should soon reach the first ranges of the Alleghany Mountains. As we had previously determined to travel in day-time across the ridges, gorges, valleys, and barren wastes of those mountains, we thought we would turn west and reverse, as soon as possible, the order of our times of sleep and travel, sleeping at night and traveling in day-time. We accordingly turned our faces to the west. By so doing we did not reach the mountains as soon as we should have done had we continued in the northward course.

We spent another night and day, March 3, 1864, in the valley between the Blue Ridge and Alleghany Mountains. Nothing deserving of particular notice transpired during that day. An hour or more before day, on the early morning of March 4th, we came to a considerable stream, washing the base of one of the principal ridges of the Alleghanies. We had been traveling the greater part of the night over a very rough and hilly road, and were getting tired and sleepy. As we expected to begin traveling in day-time over the mountains on the day then approaching, in accordance with our previous programme, we determined not to cross the stream that night, or morning rather, and followed the road back a short distance to where the woods bordered it on the south. We then left the road and entered the woods, going in a south-east course a little more than a half mile. In a spot surrounded by small trees and bushes, where the surface of the ground was covered with rock large and small, we halted for the day, March 4th. We cleared the rocks from a small space, sufficiently large for our bed. We then made it and went to rest for a few hours.

CHAPTER IV.

AWAKENED—WATCHING IN AMBUSH—AVERILL'S CAVALRY—WOMAN MAKING SUGAR—WE SEE MEN DRESSED IN BLUE—DECEIVING THE WOMAN - CHANGE OF BASE—MISLEADING PURSUERS—WE EAT LAST OF OUR SUPPLIES START OUT IN DAY-TIME IN ACCORDANCE WITH AGREEMENT—OUR DISCOVERY—OUR PURSUIT—OUR FLIGHT—TRIPPE FAILS—HE FALLS BY THE WAY—REBELS THREATEN—OUR SPEED OUR SAFETY—TRIPPE'S PROBABLE FATE.

NEAR nine o'clock, A. M., March 4th, we were awakened by the rumbling noise of a wagon running over a rough and stony road not far to the east of us. We supposed this road intersected the one we had been traveling during the night, but we had not noticed the point of intersection. On finding we were near a road upon which persons would be passing during the day Smith cautiously ventured in the direction of the road to a cluster of cedar bushes, from which, while concealed from observation, he could see any one passing. Soon another wagon was heard coming down the road. Smith watched in the bushes until the wagon passed, when he returned to us, reporting that the wagon was a common army wagon, and that the driver had on a blue overcoat. "Can it be," said Smith, "that Averill's cavalry are on a raid through here?" As we knew the Con federates wore blue coats whenever they got possession of them we did not comfort ourselves with the hope that Union troopers were in the vicinity. We rather concluded there was a squad of Confederate military in the neighborhood, and thought best to look about us a little.

Smith, having been out east of us and taken a survey of the road and adjacent woods, thought he would take a look to the south and south-west of us. Keeping under cover of the brush as much as possible, he went out south of us, intending to be gone only a few minutes. Fully a half hour passed and Smith had not returned, and, finally, we suspected something wrong, and quietly, though quickly, folded our blankets and got ready for a "skedaddle." We did not, however, intend changing our location before Smith returned, or until it was certain he would not return at all, unless somebody else came upon us in our present retreat. We had but a few minutes to wait before we saw Smith approach from the south in a brisk, though cautious walk.

"What does this mean?" asked Smith, on noticing we had torn up camp, and were looking as though we were about ready to fly.

"It means that we had given you up as lost or captured," answered Trippe.

"Well," said Smith, "I think it will be policy for us to shift from this place."

"We have been in momentary expectation of a summons to surrender," added Trippe.

Smith had gone south of our camp but little more than a quarter of a mile. He was bearing considerably to the west, when he noticed to his right, and just beyond a bluff or ledge, a smoke curling upward. Not hearing or seeing any one, he walked up to the edge of the bluff and looked over and saw a woman engaged in boiling sugar-water. As he was endeavoring to gain the shelter of the bushes the woman noticed him shying off and asked, "What are you afeared of?"

"O nothing; only I was afraid you would be scared if you saw me," answered Smith.

While conversing briefly with the woman Smith found she thought it nothing strange to have met a man dressed in blue. Just as he was on the point of asking if there were Federal soldiers near he happened to see four or five men approaching a log cabin, which was situated in the center of a cleared space of ground. Two of the men were dressed in blue; the others were clad in butternut. The cabin was quite a quarter of a mile distant to the south-west. Smith observed to the woman, "There is a company of soldiers not far from your house."

This remark was made in such a tone and manner as led the woman to believe that Smith was acquainted in the vicinity. As it was also half inquisitive, the woman answered that there was a company of soldiers not far off, and asked, "An't you one of 'em?"

Having gained the information desired, and seeing the opportunity of deceiving the woman, Smith replied, "Of course I am."

"Well," said the woman, "I thought it curious if you was n't."

"O, yes," returned Smith, "I'm a soldier."

"As there was a horse tied to a tree near the woman having a man's saddle on it, Smith expected a man—perhaps a soldier—would be there presently, and started off, observing as he left, "Well, I must go back to camp."

On leaving the woman, Smith went in a direction contrary to that which he expected to take on getting out of her sight. He soon after approached our hiding-place from the south, as before mentioned. On hearing Smith's narration of facts, as given above, we gathered our things and started eastward. On reaching the road on which the wagons had passed, we walked backward across it. We went through the woods some distance further east, and then we turned north. We soon came to the road over which we had passed during the night, and crossed it, walking backward. We continued in a northern direction until we had gone something more than a mile from the road, and had reached heavy woods with a thick bushy undergrowth, in which we halted for awhile. After a few moments' rest and consultation, we retraced our steps a short distance to a branch we had crossed, and in it we washed our hands and faces. We then eat the last of our provisions, and had nothing left to carry with us to subsist on.

Near three o'clock, P. M., having got every thing ready, we started on our travels in daylight, in accordance with previous arrangement. We made our way through the woods and brush with some difficulty, in a western direction, until we had gone about a mile, when we noticed an opening not far to our left, where the timber had been cleared away. We approached this cleared land, in order to avoid the thickets of brush. On reaching it, we saw a small log cabin in the edge of the woods, on the opposite side of it. As we saw no one, we went along near the brush and woods, going toward the stream we had encountered at day-break, before we had found our place of refuge for the day. When within two hundred yards of the stream, having gained a point directly north of the cabin, we looked toward it, and saw a woman standing near its south-west corner. As she was not looking at us, we judged she had not noticed us, and as she was almost half a mile distant, we deemed it unnecessary to change our course on her account. On reaching the bank of the stream, and before going down to the water's brink, we again looked toward the cabin, and saw that the woman was just disappearing. Almost at the same instant we heard the loud, shrill, blast of a horn or bugle. Not knowing for what purpose the bugle had been sounded, we thought it boded us no good at least. When we reached the margin of the stream we removed the shoes and socks from our feet, then putting our shoes on, we waded the stream. Wood and Trippe had reached the opposite bank, and Smith, Sutherland, and I were nearing it, when looking to our left we saw a man on horseback coming down the road that passed between the stream and the ridge of the mountain. He came toward us rapidly until he saw us plainly, when he wheeled suddenly about, and dashed back up the road with great speed. He was bare-headed, and when he turned about in the road, displaying his long locks of hair, and the cape of his overcoat, with its brass buttons glistening in the sunlight, we at once realized our situation, and the necessity of getting away from there as quickly as we could. We took time, however, to put on our dry socks; then putting our shoes on, and lacing them securely, we left the bank of the stream and the road directly in our rear, and pushed up the mountain-side as rapidly as the nature of the ground would permit.

The ridge near its base was thickly covered over with pine and cedar bushes, but as we neared its summit, the bushes were more scattering. The side of the ridge was covered over with rocks, large and small, and it was impossible to make a footprint on its stony surface. Near the top of the ridge, and on its summit, were innumerable rocks of large and massive size. Trippe having been recaptured once and sent back to prison, was determined to avoid, if possible, the recurrence of an event fraught with such calamitous consequences. On the first appearance of danger he had hurried his preparations for leaving the stream, and had started out in advance of the other four of us. We only aimed to keep Trippe in view, and allow the distance between him and ourselves to grow no greater. Trippe was within two hundred yards of the summit of the ridge when he stopped to rest. As soon as we saw he had halted, we did the same, although we were not much wearied. But we wished to husband our strength as much as possible, knowing we should be hunted and pursued. Smith, Sutherland, Wood, and I kept near together, that we might consult each other as we hurried forward, for we recognized the value and importance of concerted action in the expected emergency.

We had rested a very few minutes when we looked up the mountain and saw Trippe hurrying to the top of it. Supposing from his extraordinary exertions that he had seen pursuers from his more elevated position, we cast a glance below us. At first glance we saw no one, but thought we could see the tops of the bushes moving near the base of the ridge. We watched for a moment only, and then saw five or six bare-headed Butternut gentry appear in sight, as they emerged from the bushes, about two hundred yards below us. They had guns, with bayonets attached, but were minus their cartridge-boxes. We pushed ahead at a moderate run for the top of the mountain, occasionally looking behind us to see if the Rebels were gaining on us. On reaching the summit of the ridge we followed it, as Trippe had, in a north-eastern direction. Soon we came to a deep chasm, or gorge, through the top of the mountain. On the sides of this chasm were many large rocks, and a few scattering trees or bushes. Should our pursuers fire on us, we thought we could make it very difficult for them to hit us, by constantly dodging about, and disappearing behind the huge rocks.

As Smith, Sutherland, Wood, and I were going down the south side of the chasm, Trippe was hurrying with might and main up its north side. Just as our pursuers reached the chasm, on its south side, we gained the top of the ridge on the north of it. Should the Rebels all commence to cross the chasm at once, we should be cut of sight before they got over; so they divided their squad, two remaining to watch our movements, while the others crossed in pursuit of us. Just as we had gained the top of the ridge north of the gorge, the two Rebels on the south side of it cried out, "Halt! halt! you d—d Yankees, you, or we'll shoot you." Having little fears of bullets at such long range, and feeling sure they had but one round of ammunition with them, we paid no attention to their threats. No shots were fired at us, but threats to shoot were repeated as long as we were in hearing.

Although we had hurried considerably, we discovered Trippe was out of sight, and we increased our speed, as much to get a view of him as to gain on our pursuers. We had gone but a few yards after so doing before we came to Trippe lying on the ground, near a large crevice or opening in a huge rock. He was completely exhausted, and unable to speak or make himself understood. We scarcely halted on reaching Trippe, as three or four of the Confederates had gained the top of the ridge north of the gorge, and were yelling at us to halt and surrender. They were not more than a hundred yards distant, but many rocks of huge proportions intervened between them and ourselves. Trippe at this moment motioned to us with both arms, and then began crawling into the opening in the rock near him. What he wished us to do we did not know, and had no opportunity of ascertaining, as we were obliged to flee for our own safety. He attempted to speak but could not.

We left Trippe to his fate, and hurried on without stopping, until we were entirely out of hearing of the Rebels. When we were beyond the immediate reach of the enemy, it was a question with us whether we should pause for a few moments, to see if Trippe had escaped their notice, or push ahead. We halted and listened for a few minutes, but heard nothing. We concluded the enemy had found Trippe, and were now looking among the rocks for us, and determined to push forward. We kept on the top of the ridge for the distance of nearly two miles, when we came to a gorge leading down the western slope of the mountain into the valley. We followed down this gorge until we were fully half-way to the valley. In a place entirely surrounded by cedar bushes, we halted to rest. The sides of the gorge were high and rugged, and huge rocks projected from them, and hung almost directly over our heads. No sound fell upon our ears; not even of the wind gently blowing, or of running water's low murmur. It was truly a place of solitude. The unfortunate event of the evening, the loss of our comrade, made it doubly sad and solitary to us. As we had made very few, if any, footprints, we knew the enemy could not easily trace us; and though sorrowing and dejected in spirit, we felt safe in the loneliness and seclusion of the place. We felt deeply the loss we had sustained in our separation from Trippe, as we had hitherto deferred to him in all the straits and critical situations in which we had been placed. It was the second time he had been recaptured—if really recaptured this time—and foiled in his attempts to escape prison, and on that account we felt sorry for him. We called to mind the reluctance manifested by him to starting with us on the trip to the lines; also his great discouragement when he came across the citizen in the woods, about ten days previously. We conjectured the Rebels had certainly found Trippe. We conjectured, too, that Trippe, in motioning to us, had intended to be understood as directing us to hide, as he was doing; that the Rebels would question him as to where the rest of us were, and that he would answer that we were hid among the rocks somewhere near; that they would look for us, and, failing to find us, would accuse him of deceiving and delaying them in their pursuit of us until we were out of reach. Taking this view of the matter we feared the Rebels would become exasperated at Trippe, and would treat him cruelly, if they did not murder him. Whatever the result of the fray might have been to Trippe, we knew we were yet free. Knowing it was entirely beyond our power to rescue or protect him, we sadly realized the extent of our loss, and began to look out again for ourselves.

To this date, February, 1870, I have never heard either from or of Trippe, and know nothing as to his fate. He was about thirty-four years of age, was a man of good judgment, and possessed many excellent qualities of mind and heart. I think he had been at one time Orderly Sergeant of his Company, Company H, 15th United States Infantry. He enlisted at Columbus, Ohio, in the year 1861. He was never married.

CHAPTER V.

ACROSS RIDGE AND VALLEY—WE SEE NEW CASTLE IN THE DISTANCE—CHILDREN SCARED—WOMEN AMAZED—WE VISIT THEM—THEY THINK WE ARE "SECESH"—WE THINK THEY ARE "SECESH"—EACH PARTY MISTAKEN—ALL GOOD UNIONISTS—A DESERTER HID UNDER THE BED—HE COMES FORTH—AT "JERMES" HUFFMAN'S—HE THINKS WE ARE CONFEDERATES—FINE SUPPER AT MIDNIGHT—WE ARE BEWILDERED IN THE DARKNESS AND RAIN—DUCKED IN CRAIG'S CREEK—WE AVOID REBEL RENDEZVOUS HIDE IN THE MOUNTAINS—AT THE HOUSE OF A CONFEDERATE HOME GUARD—HE IS SICK—PROVES TO BE A UNION MAN—ONE CORN-DODGER—HE SENDS US TO ANOTHER UNION MAN—WE LOSE OUR WAY—PRECIOUS TIME LOST—WE ARRIVE AT WM. PAXTON'S—SUPPER AT MIDNIGHT—AN OLD REBEL BADLY FOOLED—PAXTON DIRECTS US TO ROBERT CHILDS'S—CHILDS NOT AT HOME—HIS WIFE PRETENDS TO BE SECESH—SHE THINKS WE ARE SECESH—CHILDS COMES HOME—HE VISITS US IN THE WOODS—HE IS A RABID SECESH—ADMITS WE ARE UNIONISTS—BUT BELIEVES THE CONTRARY—THE MYSTERY ACCIDENTALLY SOLVED—MRS. CHILDS A UNIONIST—MR. CHILDS A UNIONIST—THEY COME TO KNOW WE ARE UNION SOLDIERS—GOOD FEELING—WE ARE FED—WE ARE SENT TO DAVID HELPER—WE SEPARATE FROM CHILDS.

WE rested in the gorge for the space of half an hour. Soon after leaving it we reached the valley. We crossed the valley, and immediately began the ascent of another ridge, and on gaining its summit we could see a town in the distance to the west of us. We ascertained, late in the day, that the town was New Castle, Craig county, Virginia. We went down the mountain-side into another valley, and then changed our course, and followed up the valley in a direction a little east of north. In passing through a dense thicket we came to a dilapidated rail-fence. We crossed the fence, and soon emerged from the thicket into more open ground. We were bearing considerably to the east, following around the thicket, when we suddenly came upon a hut. Three or four children were at play near the door. They saw us and ran into the house immediately, when two women appeared at the door and gazed at us in apparent amazement. As it was growing late, the sun having gone down, we knew the women could bring no harm upon us, and we approached the humble dwelling and entered it without waiting for an invitation. We took seats, and opened the conversation by telling the women to set before us, on the table, what they had cooked, as we were hungry, and had nothing to eat. The women complied, setting out a few slices of cold boiled meat, a couple of corn-dodgers, and four bowls of milk. We sat around the table and eat all that had been placed upon it. After eating we told the women that was the first milk, with one exception, we had drank for many months, and that was the first bread we had eaten for two days.

The women seemed very much astonished, and inquired who we were, and where we were from. We told them we had been prisoners at Danville, Virginia, and were now trying to make our way through the mountains to the Union lines. They then apologized to us for the scantiness of the meal they had given us, saying they thought we were Confederate guards from New Castle. We also apologized to them for ordering them, in so abrupt a manner, to set out supper for us, saying we thought they were "Secesh." The women then called for "Jim" to come out from under the bed. "Jim" immediately came forth. On our approach he had hid under the bed, thinking we were Confederate home guards. Jim was a deserter from Buckner's army in East Tennessee. We told these Unionists of the event of the afternoon; of our being pursued, and of losing one of our number in our flight. They seemed to manifest much anxiety on account of the lost one, and asked us many questions concerning him,

We inquired if there was any good Union man living in the valley of whom we could procure provisions to carry with us. We were told that "Jeemes" Huffman lived four miles up the branch, and could furnish us with provisions. A path was pointed out to us that led up to Huffman's house. Just at dusk we bid our Union friends "good evening" and set out, intending to give Huffman a call. About half the distance had been gone over when darkness fully set in. After dark our progress was much slower in following the strange and devious pathway. Near nine o'clock, P. M., we saw the light of a fire, shining dimly through Huffman's window. We crossed a fence and followed the path a short distance up the mountain-side to the house. The door was standing open, and we entered and stood before Huffman and his wife. They were not a little surprised, and seemed doubtful as to the manner in which they should treat us. We were soon seated before the fire, however, and began to acquaint Huffman with our condition and necessities. Having heard with interest our narrative of the facts in our case the woman asked if we would have supper. We answered in the affirmative, and she went to work, and by ten o'clock, P. M., we sat down to a table bountifully supplied with food.

While eating we learned from Huffman that he lived two and a half miles from New Castle, Craig county. We learned, also, that the home guards at New Castle searched the premises of the mountaineers every two weeks for deserters from the Confederate army. When we first entered the house Huffman supposed we were home guards from New Castle, and the hesitancy on his part to avow, at first, his Union sentiments, was the result. Huffman said it had been two weeks since his house had been searched, and he was in hourly expectation of the guards. As Huffman was engaged in shelling corn, we asked of him the privilege of shelling a few ears to carry with us to eat on the morrow. This favor was readily granted, and some three or four dozens of Irish potatoes were also furnished us.

Near eleven o'clock on that night of March 4th we were ready to set out again on our travels. Huffman gave us directions how to get across Craig's Creek, and how to avoid a certain house, which he described, where a Rebel family lived, and where the home guards sometimes stopped, when out on their semi-monthly rounds. After bidding Huffman and his wife good-night, we left them, and followed, as well as we could, the directions we had received. It had become very dark and cloudy, and before we reached Craig's Creek it began raining, and we found it impossible to follow the directions Huffman had given us. But we pushed on in the darkness, and in the course of an hour we reached the stream. We found we were considerably off the track, having missed the crossing Huffman had described. We spent half an hour or more in wandering up and down the creek, looking carefully for the crossing, but failed to find it. We spent another half hour in procuring a stout staff, or stick, apiece, to be used in the stream while wading it. Having supplied ourselves, we plunged into the waters of the creek, steadying ourselves against the swift current with our sticks as best we could.

It was very dark, and the rain continued falling. To add to the difficulty of crossing, we found that the bed or bottom of the creek was very treacherous, being full of rocks and holes. We found the water very cold, and the current strong and swift. We stumbled often, and came near falling into the water, but finally got safely across, with a thorough and cold wetting. All our clothing was wet, and dripping with water, as we stood upon the bank. We took off our blouses and wrung the water from them. After re-arranging our things, we set out again in a northern direction, following up the valley. We found it necessary to walk briskly before morning, in order to excite warmth of body to dry our clothing. As we had not crossed the creek at the point where we had expected to do so, we had avoided the house which was the rendezvous of the Rebel guards. A road was soon reached, on which we walked with much energy, and the clothing next our bodies soon became dry of the dampening effects of the plunging and stumbling in Craig's Creek. Daylight having broke upon us, we began looking for a hiding-place. Owing to the ill luck attending our first day's travel, we were induced to fall back on the old plan of lying by in daytime. As there were home guards in the country, we thought we should feel safer in trusting ourselves to the friendly shelter of the woods during the day.

Day-break found us on the road where it passed between two high ridges of mountains. There was no alternative but to hide far up in the side of the ridge east of the road. We began the ascent of the ridge, and were not long in gaining its summit; and on its eastern slope we halted for the day, among the huge rocks. In a short time we cleared a space sufficiently large for our bed. Our bedding was a little damp; but as we had lost much sleep in the last twenty hours, that circumstance did not hinder us from sleeping soundly. We slept until late in the day, when we made a fire preparatory to parching corn and roasting potatoes. We eat as much as we wished of the potatoes and corn, and finding we did not much relish such fare, since the excellent though late supper at Huffman's the night before, we determined to have something better to eat the next day, if possible. We resolved that the first house we came to, after setting out, should be the scene of an attempt, at least, to get some provisions. The time of starting having arrived, and all being in readiness, we crossed the summit of the ridge and descended to the road in the valley. We walked leisurely along the road, not wishing to reach the first house too early in the night. Near nine o'clock we came to a house on our left, a short distance from us. We heard music as we halted, and questioned the propriety of entering the house; but finally concluded not to forego our resolution to try our hand at procuring supplies. We crossed the rail-fence a few steps from the house, and went to the door. We opened the door, entered the house, and took seats without waiting to be asked to do so. Four or five children were seated before the fire. The oldest, a boy about fifteen years old, had been playing the violin. As we entered the house the mother of the children stepped out the back door, but did not close it entirely. The mother held the door slightly open, and listened to what we had to say to the children. On finding we talked kindly, she came into the room, and then we made known the object of our call at such a time. The woman represented herself as being very poor, with a sick husband and five children to provide for. She pointed to the bed in the corner in which her husband lay. On looking, we saw the unfortunate man, and conversed with him. We learned he had lost his health while serving in the Confederate army under Buckner. On account of disability, he had been discharged from service, and allowed to return to his family. He now belonged to a home guard company. In the course of the conversation, the sick man claimed he was really a Union man, but had been obliged to yield to the pressure of public opinion, and had been conscripted into the army. He now belonged to the home guards, to keep from being again sent to the front. He said he would gladly give us something to eat, but as it was beyond his ability to do so, he could only direct us to a man who could provide for us. After giving us particular directions how we should find the home of William Paxton, he said no more. We bade the sick man and family "good-night," and left the house. Before we had reached the fence, one of the children opening the door called out to us to wait a minute. We waited, and the boy brought us one corn-dodger. Taking it, we expressed our thanks, and went on our way.

On getting some distance from the house, we debated as to the propriety of seeking Paxton's aid. We feared Paxton was a Rebel. It seemed strange that a late follower of Buckner, and a Confederate home guard, should give directions to escaping Federals; but as he had given us bread from his limited supply and had told us just how to avoid and get around a certain house where Confederate guards often met, we concluded to follow his directions, if possible, and if we found things as represented, we would go to Paxton's.

It was seven miles to Paxton's house, which was situated on the road as it passed over a mountain. After going some four miles on the road, we came to the house where the Rebels congregated. It was near the road, and lights shone from all the windows. We passed some distance south of it, but near enough to hear the noise of revelry. At a point nearly two miles west of this house, we should have gone on the mountain; but owing to the indistinctness of the road, and the darkness of the night, we missed our way. When we found we were off the right track, we retraced our steps for over a mile. As it was near morning we began a careful search for the point where the mountain road led off to the left from the other, and found it just at day-break. We could now do nothing but look out for a hiding-place for the day, Sunday, March 6th.

According to the account of the sick man, we were hid but little more than a mile from Paxton's abode. Our retreat for the day was close to a spring, where we could wash and get water to drink. In the evening, fearing ramblers would come to the spring, we moved further from it. Having eaten our corn-dodger the preceding night, we were obliged to resort for subsistence to the remnant of roasted potatoes and corn left over from yesterday's fare. The day seemed long, but it wore away, and we took up our line of march, near nine o'clock, P. M., for Paxton's house. In less than two hour's time we came to a house answering the description we had received. We passed through the gate in front and approached the door. We rapped gently, and were invited by an old man to come in. As we were being seated, one of our party asked the old man if his name was Paxton. He answered that it was; and wished to know how and where we had learned his name. We told him, and he seemed much surprised, as our informant had been considered by him as a disunionist. All had retired to sleep at Paxton's excepting himself. We told him we wished something to eat, and he immediately called his two daughters to get our supper for us. Paxton knew we were Federals, and made no attempt to conceal his Union sentiments. While waiting for supper, we conversed on war topics, on prison life, and our trip since leaving prison. When supper was announced, we sat down to a table bountifully supplied with food. While we were eating, an old man stopped at Paxton's, who had been out from Fincastle, where he lived, to take a woman to her home in the country. This new-comer did not seem to notice us until we had finished supper and taken seats before the fire. As I was sitting next him, he took hold of my pants at the knee, and inquired rather roughly, "Where do you belong?" Not knowing what answer to make, under the circumstances, to such a question, I merely turned my head, and glanced at my three comrades, who in turn looked immediately to the old man Paxton, who very quickly spoke up saying, "They belong to the 22d, which you know is stationed at the bridge." Paxton immediately added, "They have been home on furlough, their time is up, and they are now on their way to the bridge." The old Fincastle man seemed satisfied with Paxton's explanation. One of our party soon after observed, as he was rising from his seat, "Well, boys, we must be off now; we must put in an appearance at the bridge as soon as possible." We then gathered our things and went out of the house. As we passed out, Paxton was seating the Fincastle man at the supper table. That done, he opened the door, and said to us, "Boys, you'll find it cold traveling over the mountain to-night."

"Yes," said Wood, laughing, "but we'll only walk the faster and get to the bridge sooner."

Paxton then came out, closing the door behind him. He told us the old fellow at the supper table was a notorious Rebel. As Paxton wished to get in the house as soon as possible, to attend to his Rebel guest, thus keeping down suspicion, he told us where and how to find the house of Robert Childs, who lived eleven miles from there. Childs, he said, was a good Union man, and his wife was a true Union woman, who would be glad to help us on our way. On getting over the mountain, and reaching a point about seven miles from Paxton's, we were to turn to our right, and go north four miles to another road, on which Childs lived.

We then set out anew on the night's travel. In two hours' time we had traveled, as we thought, about seven miles, and we called at a house and inquired of a negro how far we were from the road leading north to the mill. We were told it was half a mile east of there; and without delay we hastened back on the road a short distance, and began looking carefully for the turning off place. We soon found it, and also found much difficulty ahead of us. The road, it seemed, was a new one, having been cut but recently through a heavy wood. We made slow progress; we stumbled often over stumps and rocks. The moon was shining, but its light scarcely reached our pathway, as the dense woods closely hedged it in. We trudged slowly on, and reached Childs's Mill before day-break. The mill was near the point where the road we had been following intersected another running east and west. Although it was not yet day, we concluded to call on Childs at his house, tell him our wants, and ask him to show us where we could stop for the day and be safe.

We halted opposite the house, and Sutherland went into the yard and rapped at the door, but no answer came. He next attempted to raise a window, but a woman's voice protested against it. Sutherland then inquired if Childs was at home, and the woman answered that he was not. The woman's tone of voice plainly indicated that she was considerably frightened; so we determined to seek a hiding-place in the forest. When we had found a suitable place, we made our bed and lay down on it to sleep. Morning was faintly appearing when we lay down, and we heard chickens crowing in the distance. In about two hours' time we awoke, and found the sun shining brightly. We consulted briefly as to what we should do, and determined that one of our party should go back to Childs's house, to see if he had got home, and to get something to eat, as we had brought nothing with us from Paxton's on account of the presence of the Fincastle Rebel. Each of us was anxious to perform the errand, and we drew cuts to see which of us should go upon it. It fell to my lot, and I at once started.

As it was early in the morning, I encountered no persons upon the road. On reaching the house I rapped moderately at the door. Mrs. Childs first looked at me through the window, and then admitted me. I first told her I was one of those who had called at the house before day. I then asked her if her husband had got home. She answered that he had not. I asked when she expected him. She answered that he would be at home by ten o'clock in the day. She then inquired what business we were on, and what we wanted with her husband. I told her we had been prisoners of war at Danville, and had been trying for over two weeks to make our way through the Confederacy to the Federal forces. I told her of our stopping at Paxton's, and of his directing us to Robert Childs. At this Mrs. Childs seemed surprised, and remarked that Paxton would better be in other business than giving aid to Federals. Mrs. Childs talked very much like a Rebel, and though I could hardly understand the situation, I felt no uneasiness. After further talking I asked her if she could furnish us something to eat. She said she supposed she could, but wasn't in the habit of feeding roving squads of soldiers. She then asked me to sit up to the table and eat with her; but I declined, telling her if she would allow me to carry a dishful to the woods, and share it with my comrades, I would be thankful. Mrs. Childs and her children eat their breakfast, while I sat by keeping up the talk with her. Shortly after finishing her meal, Mrs. Childs gathered what she had left on a large dish and gave it to me. I thanked her, and told her there must be a mistake somewhere, as we had found things very different from what Paxton had represented.

"Paxton don't know every thing," said Mrs. Childs.

"Time alone will settle the matter," said I. I told the woman where we were hid, and asked her to send her husband to see us when he returned. She answered that she would do so.

"If you will," said I, "we shall have a friendly talk with him, do him no harm, and send your dish back to you."

I then returned to our retreat in the woods. On the way I felt, from some cause, that Paxton was not mistaken in his opinion of Mrs. Childs, and that some recent development had made necessary her avowal of disunion sentiments. We found the provisions furnished by Mrs. Childs very acceptable, whether she was a secessionist or not. After finishing our meal we spent the time in conjecturing the cause of Mrs. Childs's strange conduct, if she was really a Union woman. We became satisfied that, for some reason yet to be explained, she had only pretended to be a devotee of the Confederacy.

Near noon Robert Childs came to us in the woods. He

approached us with extreme caution, and looked as if he would rather not see us. We talked with him an hour or more. During the whole conversation he upheld the Confederacy. He could not imagine how Paxton got the impression he was a Union man or a disloyal citizen. We asked Childs if he should take any steps to recapture us. He replied that he would do nothing either to help or hinder us. To this we replied, that we could ask no more from a "Secesh." He started home when we gave him the dish, and told him we were grateful to his wife and to him for what we had received from them. We urged Childs to call on us again before night. He said he would if he had time, and then went homeward.

Near four o'clock, P. M., he came out again to see us, and remained with us until near sunset. The tenor of his conversation was the same as in the morning. He had no word of encouragement to give us, and, of course, offered us no assistance. It was growing late, and we began getting ready to travel. We continued talking with Childs, however, and Smith said to him,

"I suppose you have n't reported us, have you?"

"I 've seen nobody to report to," he answered.

"Has n't any one been to mill?" inquired Smith.

"O, one or two," answered Childs, "but they were in a hurry, and did n't stay long?"

"You did n't say any thing about us, then?" asked Wood.

"I did n't say a word about you to any body," said Childs.

Sutherland then said, "I 'll be switched if I do n't believe he is a Union man after all."

Childs manifesting some uneasiness, then said in an emphatic manner, "Do n't fool yourselves about that, boys."

Sutherland then asked, "Did you ever see or hear of any Yankee prisoners escaping through here before?"

Childs said he had heard of a squad passing through about six weeks before.

"How many were there in the squad?" Smith inquired.

"Only two, I believe," was the reply.

"I 'll bet," said Smith, "they were Davis and Tige; they left the hospital about two months ago."

Childs seemed to evince unusual interest in this remark of Smith's. Sutherland then said, "I wonder where Davis and Tige are by this time?"

"O, they've got through before now," I replied.

"Unless they've been caught and sent back," added Sutherland.

Childs then inquired rather anxiously who Davis and Tige were. We told him who they were, where we had known them, and described them particularly. Davis had been steward at the hospital near Danville, and Tige had been a nurse. Childs then recanted his secession doctrines, and confessed he was a Union man, and had harbored Davis and Tige for three or four days. He also explained in full the reasons for his conduct toward us in pretending to be a Rebel.

It seems the Confederate commander in that district—General Echols, I think it was—had adopted a plan of ascertaining who were aiding Federal prisoners in their efforts to escape. He had dressed small squads of his men in tattered Federal uniforms, armed them with weapons concealed about their persons, and had sent them over the country to such persons as were suspected of Unionism; to whom they would apply for food and other assistance in making their way to the Union lines. These squads were called "bogus Yankees" by the Union people, who learned to keep continually on the guard against falling victims to their deceptive practices. Many true Union citizens of the South were made prisoners by the "bogus Yankees," taken from their homes, and imprisoned at Richmond, Atlanta, and other points, for many months.

Childs thought we were "bogus," and was glad enough to help us when he found the contrary was true. Paxton had not yet learned of the "bogus Yankees," and Childs had only been put on his guard a day or two before by hearing of the arrest and carrying off in irons of one of his Union friends, who had the misfortune to fall into the hands of the impostors. Childs said he would take it upon himself to go and see his friend Paxton, and warn him of the danger of playing into false hands. Robert Childs, in treating us as he had, only thought he was evading arrest and a hopeless imprisonment. He first assured himself of our genuineness; then, knowing our actual need of assistance, he did not withhold it. It was purely accidental—perhaps Providential—that our real character became known to Childs. The allusion to Davis and Tige was the merest accident in the world, but proved sufficiently powerful to dispel the mystery we had been unable to solve.

The day, March 7th, was drawing to its close. It was time for us to resume our secret march. Before we set out Childs went to his house and brought us enough provisions for one meal, which was all that we required, as he then gave us particular directions as to how we should find the house of David Hepler, another good Union man, only eight miles away. We then parted with Childs, who had so recently proved our friend, in a better mood than we had anticipated an hour before. We were sorry we could remain no longer with him after he had found us also true, and of the number in whom he could confide.

CHAPTER VI.

"HAD NO HORNS LATELY"—WE REACH HEPLER'S—HE IS ON HIS GUARD—WE KNOW HOW TO TAKE HIM—SUPPER AND LODGING—ADIEU TO HEPLER—WE GO TO LEWIS'S HOUSE—LEWIS NOT AT HOME—TROUBLE AT LEWIS'S HOUSE—ITS OCCUPANTS PROPOSE MAKING US PRISONERS—WE PROPOSE DIFFERENTLY—NEITHER PARTY ACTS—ONE-SIDED MISUNDERSTANDING—AN UNDERSTANDING NOT ATTAINABLE—WE RETURN TO HEPLER—HE DREADS TO SEE US—HE IS SOON ALL RIGHT AGAIN—HE ASCERTAINS LEWIS'S FATE—IS UNABLE TO SECURE US A GUIDE—WE ARE PRONOUNCED "SPURIOUS"—FINAL ADIEU TO HEPLER—WE RETURN TO LEWIS'S HOUSE—GET PROVISION THERE AND SOMETHING MORE—FURTHER TRAVELS—OUR MATCHES LOST—WE REACH GREENBRIER RIVER—COME UNEXPECTEDLY TO TWO WOMEN—THEY SEND US TO MRS. MANN'S—WE REST OURSELVES—VOLUNTEER GUIDE.

IT was near sunset when we separated from Childs. Just before dark we felt uncertain as to whether we had not got off the route to Hepler's. As there was a house a short distance to our left, we concluded to inquire the way, as we preferred risking a little to getting bewildered in the darkness. We found one young woman and two older ones at the house. On seeing us they seemed badly scared, and were about to forsake their dwelling as we entered it, leaving us in full possession. After some entreaty on our part, the young woman came in cautiously and deferentially, and was followed by the older ones. Our inquiries were principally addressed to the young woman, the older ones standing near gazing in mute astonishment. In the course of the talk we had occasion to acknowledge that we were Yankees, when one of the old women blurted out, "I'd say! I thought they had horns."

"We do have, sometimes," said Wood, "but not lately."

On gaining the information desired, we resumed our journey. By eight o'clock we had traversed the rough, broken country lying between Childs's and Hepler's house. We found Hepler on the look out for false Unionists; but as Childs had told us Davis and Tige had been befriended by him—Hepler—we found no difficulty in proving our genuineness to him. Near nine o'clock we took supper at Hepler's table, and after a two hours' talk, we were comfortably lodged in his house. After breakfasting the next morning, having got ready to set forth again on our journey, we bade Hepler's family adieu, and he conducted us to the top of a lofty range of mountains, at the base of which his house stood. Having reached the highest elevation in the mountain, Hepler pointed out to us another range upon which the home of William Lewis was situated. The exact locality of Lewis's house was pointed out, although we could scarcely see it, and were eight and a half miles distant. Hepler told us we could go to Lewis's in day-time without much risk, but it would be impossible for strangers to go over the route by night. He also informed us that it was probable we could get Lewis to guide us a portion of, if not all, the way to the Federal lines. On hearing some further instructions to enable us to find our way more easily, we bade our friend adieu, and left him. It was fully ten o'clock in the day when we set out on our journey to Lewis's house. We crossed two ridges, as many valleys, and many small rivulets of the mountains before reaching our objective point. On commencing the ascent of a third ridge, we found a path of which Hepler had spoken. We then knew we were on the ridge upon which we would find the house of a friend. We took the path as a guide, and followed its devious course. When little more than half-way up the mountain side we met two men and a woman and child. The men were on foot. The woman, with her child in her arms, was on horseback. The largest man was carefully leading the horse down the mountain path. No word was spoken at this meeting, each party maintaining silence and casting suspicious glances at the other. Soon after we gained the top of the ridge, and came in sight of Lewis's house, situated in a bowl-shaped depression in the top of the mountain. We did not wish to go to the house while it was yet day, for fear of finding some Secessionist there, and thus placing Lewis as well as ourselves in an embarrassing situation. We went aside from the path nearly two hundred yards, and hid in the brush. We found we had stopped in a place from which we could watch the house. Our position also commanded a view of the path we had just left, and of persons that might pass upon it.

It was near four o'clock, P. M., when we halted. We kept our eyes at intervals on the house and its immediate surroundings, but saw no person during the evening. One dog, a calf, and a few chickens, were the only living objects visible. The doors of the house were closed, and we concluded Lewis and his family had gone from home; but as smoke was issuing from the chimney, we hoped they would return by dark. We feared the man we had met leading the horse was Lewis with his family, going with a friend to make a visit. If so, we should be delayed, we thought, in our journey, and be compelled to push on without seeing him. We decided to wait until dark in our hiding-place, and see if Lewis would return. Just after sunset the man we had met on the mountain, leading the horse, went along the path to Lewis's premises. He was leading a horse, and was accompanied by two other men, each leading horses. They first put their horses in the stable and fed them. They then chopped some wood at the wood-pile and carried it to the house. Darkness came on, and we saw sparks flying from the chimney top.

Feelings of joyous gratitude heaved our bosoms as we felt certain we should soon meet Lewis and enjoy the company and consolations of a native thorough-bred Union man. We were destined to meet with disappointment, however, and to experience difficulties from which a mere allusion to Davis and Tige would not relieve us.

In less than an hour after dark we left our position in the thicket and went to the house. We knocked three times before we were told to come in. With a show of reluctance on the part of the three men, we were furnished seats near the fire. Wood, addressing the largest of the men, asked, " Your name is Lewis, I suppose?"

"No, but Lewis is a brother-in-law of mine," was the answer.

" Well, this is Lewis's house, is it?" Wood asked. " We were told it was."

" Where is Lewis?" inquired Sutherland.

" I do n't know," said the man, " he has n't been at home for several days."

" What 's your name?" continued Sutherland.

" My name is Hepler."

"Are you akin to David Hepler?" Sutherland asked.

"Yes, David Hepler is my father," replied the man, at the same time turning very pale.

Judging Hepler was fearful some great calamity had befallen his father through the agency of "bogus Yankees," I said, "You think we are Rebels," and Smith immediately added, "We have not harmed a hair of your father's head."

We assured Hepler we were real Union soldiers, honestly endeavoring to make our way from prison to our lines.

"I do n't know so well about that," said Hepler, "but as for myself, I belong to the Confederate army."

We then told him we knew he belonged to the Confederate army, and knew, too, that he was a Union man, having been informed of those facts by his father. David Hepler had told us how his son, in the earlier months of the war, had hid himself among the rocks and caverns of the mountains for more than eighteen months, and how at last he was caught by the Rebels, and conscripted into the army.

We spent some time, two hours at least, in trying to convince young Hepler we were not "bogus," but all in vain. He said he knew what he was, and supposed we knew what we were, and was going to have nothing to do with Federal prisoners, unless it would be to catch them and take them to Jim Crow's. As he spoke thus he directed our attention to a stack of guns in the corner.

"There's as many of us as there is of you," suggested Wood, "when it comes to that."

"Jim Crow's" was a small town a few miles distant, as we afterward learned.

We became satisfied that our efforts to procure assistance, or derive information from young Hepler and his associates would prove unavailing, as they refused to answer our questions as to the roads, the streams, or the nature of the country west and north of us, and refused us the shelter of the house until morning. We, however, understood the situation perfectly, knowing that the only difficulty with us was our inability to furnish satisfactory proof of our genuineness as real "Yankees." Hepler having been absent in the service, knew nothing of Davis and Tige, or of the aid his father had rendered them, and our telling him of them was of no avail. We could not establish our character as escaping Federals to the satisfaction of those who, we knew, would have been our friends could we have done so, but were compelled to leave them under the impression we were really soldiers of the Confederacy.

Near eleven o'clock that night, March 8th, we left the house of Lewis not a little discomfited. Where we had expected assistance and encouragement we met only with disappointment and defeat. We felt our defeat more keenly in consequence of the certainty we felt that Hepler and his associates would have been quite willing, even anxious, to aid us on our way had they been assured beyond a doubt as to our real character.

After we had gone out of the house we halted at the fence, a few steps from the door, and consulted briefly as to the course

"TROUBLE AT LEWIS'S HOUSE."—PAGE 93.

to pursue. Our situation was critical in the extreme. We were in Alleghany county, in the midst of the rugged and barren mountains, where the country was thinly inhabited. We had no supplies with us, as we had left David Hepler's expecting to get food at Lewis's. We soon determined to return to David Hepler's, tell him of the situation at Lewis's house, and see if he could give us other directions to follow. Smith suggested that young Hepler might be willing to go with us to his father if we should wait until morning. Smith called to him to come out, saying; "We wish to talk with you."

Hepler did not come out; but on being called the third time he came to the door and said, "Kill me in the house if you want to; I sha'n't come out there to be killed."

We were trying to assure him that we would do him no harm when he closed the door in our faces and barred it. We then started away from the house, going about a mile east of it. Near the mountain top we halted until daylight of March 9th. The sky was overcast with clouds, threatening rain, when we stopped, and we felt very much disheartened. Our hopes were exultant before going to Lewis's house. We expected to get assistance there, and possibly a guide to conduct us on our way; but all had failed. We felt we had been turned empty away from the house of a friend, and Nature it seemed was about to frown on us. We came near regretting the start we had made from prison. One consolation, however, was left us; if there was any change in our prospects it would be for the better.

We made preparations for sleep, but there was little sleep for us that night. Before day rain commenced falling, and we were obliged to fold our blankets, to keep them as dry as possible. We leaned against trees, and so disposed our coats over our shoulders as to shed most of the rain off until daylight. As soon as we could see our way plainly we set out on our return to David Hepler's. We had a very disagreeable time in walking over the mountains in a drenching rain shower. We reached Hepler's just at twelve o'clock. We found him at home. He was very much surprised, even astonished, at seeing us again. He even dreaded to see us, as he at once concluded his time had come to surrender himself a prisoner into the hands of sham Yankees, his country's worst enemies. We soon explained to him the reason for our return, telling him all that had transpired since separating from him the morning before. He immediately conjectured that Lewis had fallen a victim to "bogus Yankees," and said he would go to-morrow to see his son, with whom we had met at Lewis's house, and ascertain what had become of him. After taking dinner with Hepler's family we went some distance up the mountain-side and hid ourselves among the rocks. The rain continued; but we could not shelter under Hepler's roof, as it would not do, either for Hepler or ourselves, to be found there by Rebel citizens. Near night our suppers were brought to us by Hepler. Soon after dark we took refuge from the storm in a small log hut near the road, which passed through Hepler's premises. Early in the morning of March 10th we breakfasted at Hepler's table, and soon after hid for the day among the rocks of the mountains. At noon our dinner was brought to us by Hepler's wife and daughter.

At night Hepler brought our suppers out, and reported the information he had received from his son concerning Lewis. As had been conjectured, a squad of Confederates had called at Lewis's house, and solicited his services as a guide to conduct them to the Union lines. As they were dressed in blue, and represented themselves as Federal prisoners trying to escape, Lewis consented to conduct them as far as Greenbrier River. After the necessary preparations, he started with them from his house, and, when only a few hundred yards away, these "bogus Yankees" suddenly presented their revolvers and made him their prisoner. His captors conducted him to White Sulphur Springs, and from that place he was sent, in company with three or four others, under a strong guard, to Richmond.

David Hepler's son was a brother-in-law of Lewis. At the time we were at Lewis's house, young Hepler and those with him had come there to get the household goods belonging to the family, intending to carry them over the mountain on horses the next morning. It was young Hepler, with Lewis's wife and child, accompanied by another person, that we had met on the mountain. Mrs. Lewis and her child, and the plunder, were moved to her father's house, to remain during her husband's captivity, or longer if he died. Had young Hepler known we were not "bogus," and not trying to deceive him, we could have had all the provisions we desired when at Lewis's house, and could have been sheltered there until morning. But, unhappily, we had been unable to convince him of our honesty of purpose, and as he was determined to avoid the calamity which had befallen his brother-in-law, he felt obliged to deny us all "aid and comfort."

In the evening of March 10th the rain ceased and the weather became cooler. On the morning of the 11th the mountains were covered with snow. During the day the snow melted away, and the mountain streams became swollen and almost impassable. While waiting for the waters to subside, we mended our shoes and other clothing, and washed our shirts. The pegs and other materials for cobbling were furnished by Hepler. We parched a quantity of corn, to carry with us on going forth anew on our journey. During our stay Hepler tried to procure a guide to conduct us to the lines, but failed. One man whom he tried to enlist in our behalf, although a good Union man, refused to have any thing to do with us, alleging we would yet prove spurious. Hepler would have guided us as far as the Greenbrier River, had not his aged parents, who were in a feeble condition, been under his care.

On the morning of March 12th we took leave of Hepler and his family. In our most cheerless hour of adversity we had found with them a harboring place. They befriended us when we were encompassed by enemies and suspected by friends. During the days of rain and snow, and swollen streams, we incurred a debt we can not easily repay. We are under lasting obligations to them. Having been provided with sufficient food to last us two days, we set out for the lines afresh. Hepler could send us to no one who could direct us on our way, and we went westward until we came to Lewis's house. We reached it before three o'clock in the evening. We watched in its vicinity for over an hour, and saw no one; not even the dog, the calf, or smoke curling from the chimney, could be seen as when we had watched it before. We went to it, and finding the doors securely fastened, we judged there was something inside worth looking after. We thought we might get a supply of provisions that would partially compensate us for the disappointment of our first visit to the house. We entered it through the window, and levied on all we could find that would do to eat. A small sack nearly full of meal, a cup of salt, a part of a ham of meat and a ham of venison, were obtained as the fruits of our seizure. We got out of the house with our commissary stores, taking an iron pot with us, and went west about a mile into a gorge through which ran a small stream of water. Here we halted, built a fire, and made mush by the quantity. After eating to our satisfaction, we had enough left for breakfast the next morning. By ten o'clock that night we had made our arrangements for a comfortable sleep. We rested well.

With the first dawning of morning light on the 13th, Wood and Sutherland returned to Lewis's house and got four case-knives, one for each of our party, a file, and a tin cup. The file we thought would be of use in loosening canoes or in opening smoke-houses as a last resort in procuring food. We completed our preparations for the day's travel, and were on our way shortly after sunrise. The country traversed was very rough and mountainous, being little more than a barren waste. It would have been impossible for us to have made our way over it in the night-time. We saw no person during the day. When following high ridges we occasionally saw huts and houses in the valley on either side below us. Sometimes we could see smoke when the house or chimney from which it came was concealed. Just after sunset we halted in a depression of the ridge we had been following, prepared our suppers, and made ready for the night's rest. As near as we could estimate, we had traveled during the day about fourteen miles in a north-west course. The night was passed in quiet sleep.

On the morning of the 14th we awoke before day. On getting up we rebuilt our fire, and hastily prepared our breakfast. Soon after we were equipped for our day's journey. We were in excellent spirits. We could but contrast our feelings with those we had experienced in the early morning, after our signal disappointment at Lewis's house. Then we were discouraged and baffled, now we were cheerful and hopeful. The sky was clear, the air was pure and bracing, and we made good progress. We traveled quite fifteen miles in a direction a little north of west, over the ridges, valleys, and streams of the mountain districts. At night we halted in the valley, where water was convenient. After making a fire, we spent an hour or more in preparing and eating our suppers. Our sleep during the night was refreshing.

Before sunrise on the 15th we had finished our breakfast. Our provisions were not yet exhausted, and there was no need of running any risks in replenishing our stock. We traveled only about six miles before discovering that the country became more open and more thickly settled. It was prudent for us to go no further in day-time. We accordingly looked about for a safe retreat for the residue of the day. After finding a place in the woods in which we thought we could trust ourselves, we devoted the greater part of the day to sleep, as we expected to travel at night. Just at dark we were ready to move. The first thing necessary on settihg out was to find a road on which to travel. Our journeyings of the past three days had been off the roads, across mountains and valleys, in a rough, broken country, almost inaccessible to travelers except on foot or on horseback. We found much difficulty in finding a road that would lead us aright. We kept on the move, however, taking care that our steps should be toward the goal we wished to gain.

A little after midnight we halted, as the sky became cloudy, and we could not see our way plainly before us. We went some distance north of the last road we had been following, and made our bed in the woods. Very soon after lying down we fell asleep. On waking up on the morning of the 16th, we found the ground covered with snow. Getting up we found the air very cool. We set about collecting suitable material for building a fire, but on searching for our matches we found we had lost them. As it was too cool for comfort without briskly exercising ourselves, we determined to set out in a northern direction.

After getting our things in readiness we started through the woods. We had proceeded but little more than a mile before we reached an open space. In crossing it we noticed not far to our left, just beyond the crest of a hill, a small log cabin. Smoke was issuing from the mud and stick chimney and curling gently upward. After a moment's deliberation we concluded we should hazard little in visiting the tenants of this humble abode and warming at their fire. We did so, and found the two women and one boy whom we found there to be friendly and disposed to make us comfortable. While waiting half an hour for a warm breakfast we learned we were in Greenbrier county, and within three miles of the Greenbrier River. Having ascertained that the folks were Unionists, we questioned them concerning the people in the surrounding country. We learned that the Rebel element held sway and that the few Union people were obliged to keep their sentiments to themselves.

Breakfast over, we set out again on our travels. Before leaving the cabin we discovered that snow had commenced falling. We had not gone far until the large flakes almost blinded us as they fell. We felt certain no one would be out on such a wintery day, and we thought we should incur but little risk in pushing forward to the river. Near ten o'clock we reached it, and began looking up and down the bank for a canoe in which to cross. After the snow had almost ceased falling, we were passing through a sugar-camp and came suddenly to two women, who were turning the troughs over. As they had seen us plainly, we being within a few yards of them when we first noticed them, we did not try to avoid them. We approached nearer the women, and one of our party made some observation on the state of the weather, and Sutherland added, "It's a bad day to be out." One of the women, smiling, answered, "I'll guess you are out a good piece from home."

On being questioned further, we told the women who we were, where we were from, and the point we were aiming to reach. They told us their "men folks" were in the Kanawha Valley, which was within the Union lines. We were not long in assuring ourselves that the women, as well as their "men folks," were strong Unionists. We were invited to the house. We accepted the invitation, and were soon seated before the fire, where we remained for a few minutes. Just before noon the women told us they were poor and unable to furnish us a meal, but Mrs. Mann, who lived about a mile back from the river, was not only able, but willing to keep us over until the following night, if we wished to stop so long as that. The eldest woman had already gone to Mrs. Mann's to see if any Secessionists were there. She soon returned, accompanied by two of Mrs. Mann's little boys, who were to conduct us by an obscure way to their mother's house. As no one was at Mrs. Mann's, we started immediately to her house, her boys leading the way. These boys were quite young—aged about nine and eleven years—but seemed to understand perfectly the necessity of our keeping out of sight of the Rebels.

We arrived at the house of Mrs. Mann by one o'clock. A little after two o'clock we took dinner. The dinner reminded us of the days gone by, and made us think we were almost home again. After dinner we conversed at length with Mrs. Mann and her family, treating mainly of the war as it affected the Union people of the South. Mrs. Mann had been despoiled of much property during the war by Confederates; and soon after the breaking out of hostilities her husband had been arrested because he would not forsake his Union principles. He had been imprisoned at Richmond, where, after lingering a few months, he died.

In the evening a man was seen approaching the house. When he was near enough to be recognized it was ascertained that he was a Rebel, and we were sent upstairs forthwith, to remain there until he should leave. We were detained nearly an hour upstairs, when the "Secesh" having taken leave, we were permitted to come down, and were interrupted no more that evening.

A little after dark we had supper. Soon after supper we began our preparations for setting forth on our way, but Mrs. Mann urged us to stop until the following night. As we were considerably worn and fatigued, we decided, after a short consultation, to do so. We passed the night of March 16th in Mrs. Mann's haymow. We could not stop in the house for the reason that a Rebel doctor from Frankfort was expected there that night to see a sick child. On the morning of the 17th, after the doctor had gone, we returned to the house for breakfast, and remained there during the day. When any one was seen coming we went upstairs, being very careful not to leave any caps behind to excite inquiries.

About four o'clock, P. M., a young man called at Mrs. Mann's, who belonged to a Union family west of the river. He offered to conduct us, after dark, to a man who would guide us some distance on our way, and give us directions to follow which would lead us to Gauley River. We eagerly accepted the offer. Our delay of twenty-four hours, it seemed, was going to prove profitable. We had supper just at dark, and soon after our preparations for the journey were complete. Our haversacks were filled with food sufficient to last us two or three days. We tendered our sincere thanks to Mrs. Mann and family for generous treatment received, and bade them farewell.

CHAPTER VII.

ARE GUIDED BY NIGHT TO ALDERMAN—ALDERMAN CONDUCTS US TWENTY MILES NEXT DAY—GIVES US PLAIN DIRECTIONS—RETURNS HOME—WE FIND ALDERMAN'S BROTHER-IN-LAW, WHO PUTS US ON THE NORTH SIDE OF GAULEY RIVER—WE FOLLOW DOWN GAULEY RIVER—PASS THROUGH SUMMERVILLE—COME IN CONTACT WITH AN IRISHMAN—RECEIVE ADVICE FROM HIM AND FOLLOW IT—WE REACH THE PICKETS AT GAULEY BRIDGE—WE RECUPERATE AT CAMP REYNOLDS—GO TO CINCINNATI, OHIO—GO HOME ON FURLOUGH.

OUR volunteer guide mounted his horse and started to the ford, some distance up the river, to cross it, while we were conducted to a point below, where there was a canoe, by Mrs. Mann's two boys. On reaching the river, and being told by the boys to fasten the canoe to the opposite shore, we said "good-by" to them, and set about crossing. In about twenty minutes, after running aground two or three times, and being compelled to get out into the water to set the canoe afloat again, we landed on the opposite bank. After securing the canoe, we took our shoes and socks off, drained the water from our shoes and wrung our socks dry. We then put on our socks and shoes, and laced the latter securely, and hastened to join our guide at the point previously agreed upon. We were soon on the way, our guide on horseback going some distance in advance on the road. In little more than an hour we reached the home of our guide. We waited close by for a few minutes while he put his horse away. He then conducted us on foot to a point within a mile of James Alderman's house, and then he returned homeward.

Following instructions we had received, we soon reached the house of the man whose services as a guide we expected to secure to conduct us on our journey. As we approached it the dogs set up a furious barking. Mrs. Alderman soon succeeded in quieting the dogs, and we entered the house. On seeing no one but the woman, we asked where Alderman was. The woman said he wasn't at home, and she didn't know exactly where he had gone. We made known our object in calling at such a late hour in the night, it being near midnight. Mrs. Alderman was evidently alarmed at our coming. She wished to know how we learned that Alderman lived there. We told her a young man named Gillilan had piloted us to the foot of the ridge, and directed us how to find the house. We told her further that the young man had informed us her husband would conduct us a portion of the way to the Union lines. The woman's fear seemed to be allayed on hearing this, and she stepped out the door and called her husband. Mr. Alderman soon made his appearance, but acted as if he was not sure we were there on an honest errand. When his dogs commenced barking he had hurried out of bed, and gone to the woods to secrete himself—as he had often done before—from the Confederate guards, who were on the watch for him to impress him into the service. Our business was soon made known to Alderman, and he consented to conduct us as far on our way as we could travel by four o'clock the next day.

It was after midnight when we made our bed on the floor of Alderman's cabin, to rest until the light of the 18th dawned. By sunrise we had breakfasted, and were on the way, Mr. Alderman going ahead of us several steps. Alderman carried his flint-lock gun with him, saying he "might shoot something before he got back." We suggested the risk in traveling by daylight, but Alderman said he would take us over a route where we would be seen by none but good Union people. By one o'clock we reached a house where lived a family named Ramsey. We took dinner with them. Shortly after two o'clock we set out again on the way. One of the Ramseys gave us a letter to be left at a point twenty miles east of Gauley Bridge, known as the Twenty-mile House. By four o'clock we had reached the small stream called Cherry Run, where we halted under a temporary shed which had been erected by hunters for shelter. We had no matches, and Alderman struck fire with his knife from the flint of his gun and kindled a fire for us. After receiving from Alderman particular directions how to find his brother-in-law's house, on the north side of Gauley River, he left us, saying he "must be at home by midnight."

We had traveled twenty miles, and had stopped for the night in a dense forest, several miles from any house. In all directions from our hiding-place the ground was deeply marked by narrow paths made by deer going back and forth for water. We made our supper on the supplies brought from Mrs. Mann's. We were in a place where we would not be likely to be seen, and we kept our fire burning until late in the night. Being surrounded by dense and darkening woods, with nothing to break the almost perfect stillness of the night but the murmurs of the little brook near us, we felt very lonely, more so than we had felt before on our travels. By ten o'clock we were soundly sleeping.

We awoke at the break of day on the morning of March 19th. We breakfasted early and were on the way by sunrise. We had only to follow down Cherry Run to its mouth at Cranberry Creek, and then follow down Cranberry Creek until we came to a road crossing it and running on its west side to Gauley River. The ford on Cranberry Creek was reached before three o'clock in the evening. We secreted ourselves in the woods south of the road and east of the creek until after dark, when we could travel the road in safety. The greater part of the evening was passed in sleep. On waking we snatched a hasty meal, and made ready for further travels. Soon after dark we were on the way. In due time we were wading Cranberry Creek at the ford, having first taken off our shoes and socks. We found the water very cool, and a little more than ankle deep. As soon as we got on our socks and shoes we set out on the road for Gauley River. The road led to a ferry on the Gauley, near the mouth of Cranberry Creek. It lacked nearly two hours of daylight when we reached the ferry. We went up Gauley River until we came to Cranberry Creek. We then partially stripped ourselves and waded Cranberry Creek to its east side. We found the water much deeper and the current stronger than when we had crossed it early in the night.

After dressing ourselves, we went on up the river nearly a mile further, and halted in the woods to await the dawn of day. We had not long to wait. As soon as we could see our way we started on up the river. Soon we noticed a smoke over the river, rising through the woods, and a few more steps brought us to a point from which a house could be seen. We gave two or three loud hallooes, and a man came out of the house and toward the river. A few moments more and he was in his canoe and half across the stream. As he neared the shore on which we stood we asked, "Are you a brother-in-law to Alderman?" He said he was, and we exclaimed, "All's right," with feelings of exultation. We were soon set across, and the sun was just rising when we sat down to breakfast.

After breakfast we went to the woods north of the house and hid away for the day, March 20th. At noon we returned to the house for dinner. Our host stood in the yard while we were eating, to notify us of the approach of any one, so we might slip into the brush adjoining the yard and hide. We were not molested, however, and after making arrangements with our host—whose name we can not now recall—to furnish us at our hiding-place enough food for two or three meals, we left the house. Just at sunset, according to arrangement, we received supplies. Our host informed us that his house was forty-eight miles east of Gauley Bridge, and twelve miles from Summerville, the county seat of Nicholas county. We were also told that the road leading from the ferry ran down Gauley River, through Summerville, and by the Twenty Mile House, to Gauley Bridge. where the nearest Union pickets were posted. Our things having been put in readiness, we started out just at dark on our travels. In a half hour's time we were upon the road, and making reasonable progress in a western direction.

A little after midnight we reached the suburbs of Summerville. No lights were anywhere to be seen. Every thing was still. We stopped and listened carefully for a few moments, when, hearing nothing, we advanced briskly through the town on the main road. We kept a keen lookout on either side of us as we passed through the place. The town seemed fully half burnt down. On reaching its western borders we again halted and listened, but all was quiet as before. We supposed the place might be, at least, a harboring place for scouts. On starting we pushed forward rapidly, traveling four miles, if not more, by day-break. During the last hours of the night the weather was quite cold, and the early morning was frosty.

At daylight, on the morning of the 21st, the road was leading us through an open country. Ahead of us, over a half mile distant, were woods, through which the road passed. We intended halting for the day as soon as we gained the shelter of the woods, and we pushed on briskly. Just ahead of us, inside an inclosure and beyond a turn of the road, were a few scattering trees. Among the trees were two or three hay-stacks. After getting around the turn of the road, and just as we were leaving the stacks in our rear, we discovered an aged man pitching hay to his sheep. As he was staring at us, we accosted him with, "How are you, old fellow?" The old gentleman was an Irishman, and it was only with close attention we could understand what he said. We luckily found him strong in his attachment to the Union, and too old, as he said, to change his principles. He evinced much interest in our welfare, and readily answered all our inquiries. He told us it was only twenty-eight and a half miles to Gauley Bridge, and that Captain Ramsey's Union Scouts were patrolling the country between that place and Summerville on both sides of Gauley River. He assured us it would be perfectly safe to travel the road that day provided we did not stop short of the pickets at night. Rebel citizens would make no attempt to capture us in day-time, we were told, but should they see us hiding for the night they would most likely collect a party and take us prisoners. We decided, after consulting briefly, to push on, at least to the woods, now only a quarter of a mile distant. As we started the old man said, "Go on to the bridge, boys, and you'll be safe; do n't stop outside the pickets." We did not suspect the old man of intending to get us into trouble, and his last injunction fully established our faith in his Unionism.

On reaching the woods we stepped aside from the road to consider further upon the propriety of going on. We dreaded to be retaken on the eve of entering the lines, and we determined to avoid such a calamity, if possible. We had twenty-eight miles to travel before our safety would be assured. Since we had already traveled twenty miles without rest or sleep, the question was, Can we reach the picket-post by dark? Our resolution to push on, and reach the goal for which we had been so long striving, was soon formed. We immediately started, and in little more than a half hour's time we came to a house on our right. As it was near the road we went to it and asked for breakfast, thinking we needed something in addition to what we had to strengthen us, in view of the journey to be accomplished that day. We were denied breakfast at first, and had started away from the house. As we were passing out the gate one of our party observed, "That's a pretty way to treat prisoners that's been half starved." The old lady overheard the remark and called us back. She first assured herself we were escaping prisoners, and then set before us what she had cooked. She apologized for refusing at first to give us a breakfast, saying she thought we were some of the scouts from Gauley Bridge, who too frequently applied for meals. We were informed it was not uncommon to see "blue coats" passing, which caused us to feel less uneasiness, as we thought we should not be molested on our way.

On finishing our breakfast we set out again, having only five miles to travel before reaching the Twenty Mile House. We arrived at the place by ten o'clock. We called at the principal house and left the letter we had brought from Greenbrier county. The lady to whom it was addressed happened to be in the house, and was exceedingly well pleased to receive it. Many questions were asked us concerning the affairs and people in Greenbrier county, but as our information was limited we could answer but few of them. After learning the time of day and receiving a biscuit apiece, we went on our way. We had eight hours or more in which to travel twenty miles, and we pressed on with exultant hopes. The soles of our shoes had worn considerably, and were too thin to afford adequate protection to our feet in walking over a stony road. As a consequence our feet became very sore. Smith once concluded he would be obliged to stop, and more than once fell far behind. On coming to a stream of water, Sutherland, Wood, and I, while waiting for Smith to catch up, removed our shoes and socks from our feet and waded it. We found the cold water improved our feet wonderfully. Smith soon came up in any thing but a pleasant mood, and was much disheartened besides. He thought we "must be in a hurry, keeping so far ahead all the time." We answered we were in no hurry, and Wood added, "We had forgot a cavalry-man could n't stand marching." We told Smith to pull off his shoes and socks and wade the stream. He complied, but his feet were so very sore he occupied several minutes in crossing.

On getting our shoes on we again pushed forward slowly. At the first house we came to after fording the stream, we inquired the distance to Gauley Bridge. "Five miles and a half," was the answer given us. The sun was more than two hours high, but now the journey seemed more doubtful and difficult of accomplishment than the journey of twenty-seven miles had seemed in the morning. We pressed on, however, and in the

"OUT OF THE WOODS." PAGE 107.

course of an hour we met a man of whom we asked, "How far is it to the pickets?" "Nearly three miles," was the reply. Our feet were sore, our limbs were weary, but our flagging spirits revived, and we persistently urged ourselves onward. The sun had almost run its daily course. The distance to be gone over, before our twenty-four-hour's march was accomplished, was gradually growing less. At length the picket-guard was reached, and our goal won; but the sun had gone down and the stars were appearing. As the twilight was passing into night we approached the sentinel in the road who came out to meet and welcome us. Giving each of us a hearty shake of the hand, he said, "I know where you are from; will you have some coffee?" We replied that we could not object, and were assured there was plenty of it at the Company quarters.

Although we were nearly worn down, almost exhausted, in fact, from the effects of twenty-four hours of constant wakefulness and travel, we felt an indescribable but silent ecstasy of joy and thankfulness for our deliverance from the rigorous and pinching destitution of Confederate prisons. But in the height and fullness of our heart-felt rapture, we did not forget Taylor and Trippe, the early companions of our journey. We thought it possible they had perished, but hoped they had been more fortunate than ourselves. Very soon after passing the pickets we went, in company with two or three soldiers of Companies I and H, 5th Virginia Infantry, to their quarters in the old town of Gauley Bridge, where supper, consisting of bread, meat, and coffee, was provided us. After supper we visited Captain Dixon, of Company I, 5th Virginia, in his quarters, he having sent for us.

Companies I and H, 5th Virginia, under command of Captain Dixon, were stationed at Gauley Bridge as an outpost from Camp Reynolds, which was below the falls of the Kanawha. We remained at the quarters of Captain Dixon during the night of March 21st. We did not retire for sleep until a late hour. From Dixon we first heard the particulars of the battle of Mission Ridge, in which our Companies had participated. We told Dixon of the number and condition of the prisoners about Danville, and of the strength and disposition of the Rebel garrison there.

On March 22d we went to Camp Reynolds, where we remained two days, during which time we were furnished by the soldiers and their officers with entire suits of clean clothing. In the evening of March 23d each of us wrote a letter to our respective homes, to let the folks know we were alive, and once more within the Union lines. Our feet having recovered from their soreness, we went next day, in company with three or four soldiers who were going home on veteran furlough, to Charleston, Virginia. On the 25th we got aboard a steamer, the "Victress No. 2," and went down the Kanawha to Gallipolis, Ohio, arriving there on the day following. On the 28th, having stopped over Sabbath in Gallipolis, we boarded the steamer "C. T. Dumont," and went down the river to Cincinnati. At ten o'clock, A. M., March 29th, we landed at Cincinnati, and immediately reported at Post Head-Quarters, Colonel Swayne, 99th Ohio, commanding.

After a brief talk with Colonel Swayne, and other officers at Head-Quarters, we were told to go to the Soldiers' Home and get our dinners, and then return. We started, and had got but a few steps from Head-Quarters when the sentinel at the door called out to us to come back, that the Colonel wished to speak to us. Sutherland, Smith, and I waited on the street, while Wood went to see what the Colonel wanted. Swayne asked Wood if he would like a furlough, and Wood answered he would. The remainder of our party were called in from the street, and asked the same question, to which we answered in the affirmative. Furloughs were immediately filled out, signed by the Post commander, and forwarded to Columbus, Ohio, to be approved by General Heintzleman, the Department commander. We went to the Soldiers' Home, got our dinners, and by two o'clock reported again at Head-Quarters, where we received orders to report at Lytle Barracks. Each of us was furnished with a pass good for five days and nights, giving us the freedom of the city.

On reaching Lytle Barracks we gave Colonel Swayne's order to the Captain commanding. The order required him to admit us to the barracks; to issue us the full allowance of rations; to issue us clothing, if we desired it; and allow us to pass in and out at all times of day and night until nine o'clock, P. M. On the afternoon of the 29th we made out partial descriptive lists, and drew new clothing, a full suit each, the next morning. On the 30th, after washing and dressing ourselves, we went out into the city. On the morning of the 31st our furloughs came from Columbus, approved. With our furloughs we received transportation papers. Early in the day, Wood took the train and was off for his home in Western Pennsylvania. Wood, although a resident of Pennsylvania, had enlisted in the 26th Ohio Volunteers. Later in the day, Smith and Sutherland left together for their homes in Michigan. On being left alone of our party, I went to H. H. Hills's drug store, and remained there over night with a friend, from whom I learned for the first time of the sad losses my Company had sustained in battle at Chickamauga. On April 1st I took breakfast at the Indiana House, and very soon after was aboard the cars and homeward bound. I arrived home in Georgetown, Illinois, Sunday evening, April 3, 1864, and found my letter written at Camp Reynolds, Virginia, had not been received. My visit was unexpected, and the first intimation my father and folks had received for many weeks that I was yet alive, was when I entered the old home. The letter came the next morning, April 4th.

CHAPTER VIII.

CONCLUSION—STRANGE CIRCUMSTANCE—WE BRING GLAD TIDINGS—ARE HOSPITABLY TREATED—THE END.

AS a conclusion to the foregoing imperfect sketches, we will briefly narrate an incident which happened after our arrival within the lines. On March 23d, at Camp Reynolds, while we were writing letters home, a soldier named Gasper came into the quarters where we were. As soon as we were at leisure he asked,

"Are you the boys that came in from prison two days ago?"

One of our party answered we were. Gasper then said he

had just been writing a letter to an old friend in Cincinnati, whose son was supposed to have been killed at Chickamauga, and hearing we had been captured in that battle, he thought he would inquire if we knew any person among the prisoners named Jack Phillips.

"Jack Phillips," repeated Smith, "certainly, I know him."

"Is it possible!" said Gasper.

"He was in the same prison with me, and in the same mess," said Smith.

"He lived in Cincinnati, did he, and belonged to Company — — Regiment, Ohio Volunteers?" asked Gasper. (I have forgotten the Company and Regiment to which Phillips belonged.)

"Yes, sir," said Smith, "we are talking of the same Jack Phillips." Smith went on, and described Phillips as to size, height, appearance, and general characteristics.

"Same fellow," said Gasper, "but his captain reports seeing him fall in battle."

"No doubt of that," said Smith, "I have heard Jack tell how he was stunned by a ball grazing his forehead, cutting the skin, and leaving a small scar after healing."

"The captain said Jack's forehead was bleeding when he saw him fall," remarked Gasper.

Gasper concluded Smith's former fellow-prisoner and messmate was the son of John Phillips, of Cincinnati, to whom he was just writing, and said he would finish his letter by giving the old man the information Smith had furnished concerning his son. Gasper then left us, but returned in the course of an hour, saying he had not yet mailed his letter. He wished us to promise to call on Mr. Phillips if we passed through Cincinnati. We told him we did not know that Cincinnati would lie in our route, but should we get there, in our travels, we would call on Mr. Phillips if he would give us some clew as to where we might find him. Gasper did not know the street on which Mr. Phillips did business, but thought it was somewhere near the Public Landing. He had also forgotten the street on which Mr. Phillips's residence was situated. We, however, promised Gasper to inquire for Mr. Phillips if we visited Cincinnati, and if we happened to learn either his residence or place of business, to call on him and corroborate the statements made in the letter to him. On leaving us Gasper said he would put in a postscript, telling Mr. Phillips of us, and of our promise to inquire for him if we visited Cincinnati. Gasper was seen no more by us, and we gave but little thought to the errand with which he had charged us, as we had no idea what route we should take in rejoining our commands.

It was the 30th of March, after we had dressed ourselves anew, when Smith came to me in Lytle Barracks, saying, "Where's Wood and Sutherland?"

"Gone to the city," I answered.

Smith then said, "Suppose we go into the city, look around, and make a few inquiries for the old man Phillips."

"Agreed," said I; "there is one chance in a thousand that we may find him."

We then went into the city, passing up one street and down another. Wherever sight or curiosity led us we went. We had wandered over the city, or a great portion of it, going into many shops and stores, with scarcely a thought of Phillips; but at length we came to a corner from which the river and many steam-boats lying at the wharves could be seen. Smith stood still until I came up, when he said, "Here is the Public Landing."

"It looks much like it," I replied.

Smith then asked, "Did n't that man at Camp Reynolds say that Phillips did business near the Public Landing?"

"I believe he did," said I, after reflecting. "Suppose we go in here and inquire for him."

We stepped in at the first door. It was a confectioner's establishment, and there were several men in the room. We looked into the show-cases and at other objects of interest, when presently all left the room except one elderly looking man and ourselves. Just as the old man was filling the stove with coal I approached him and asked, "Is there a person doing business anywhere in this part of the city named John Phillips?" As the old man set his coal bucket down he said, "My name is John Phillips." It was the first inquiry we had made and would have been the last, as we were anxious to get back to the barracks for dinner. After our surprise had subsided somewhat the old gentleman wished to know what we wanted. We told him of our promise to a man at Camp Reynolds, Virginia, and asked if he had received a letter from a man by the name of Gasper. He answered that he had not. After telling him we had been prisoners of war, and had come into the lines at Gauley Bridge about a week before, Smith went on to tell him all he knew about "Jack Phillips" as a prisoner at Danville, Virginia.

On hearing Smith's account of Jack, the old gentleman, bursting into tears, said he had long since given his son up as dead, and could hardly hope or believe he was yet alive; at least he should not tell the news to his family, for fear the man we spoke of might be another of the same name. Smith thought there could be no mistake, as it would not be likely to happen that two of the same name should enlist in the same regiment from the same city. "Strange things sometimes happen in this world," observed Mr. Phillips. The old gentleman wished us to eat some cakes and pies and drink some wine, of which there seemed to be an abundance in the room. We consented, as it was noon, and would save us a walk to the barracks for dinner. Just as we had finished eating, a man entered the room holding several letters in his hand, two of which he handed to Mr. Phillips. On opening the first letter Mr. Phillips found it to be the one Gasper had written at Camp Reynolds, Virginia. The coincidence caused Mr. Phillips to conclude his son must yet be alive, and he determined to acquaint his family with the news he had received. The letter coming to hand, telling about us, while we were present to answer for ourselves, and our addressing our first, last, and only inquiry for Mr. Phillips to Mr. Phillips himself, in a great city, where there were thousands of people, seemed strange, and forbade the suspicion that our report was untrue. Mr. Phillips invited us to call on him each day during our stay in the city. We called on him the next day, March 31st, which was our last day in Cincinnati. I have since learned—though indirectly—that "Jack" afterward died as a prisoner, either at Danville, Virginia, or Andersonville, Georgia.

HISTORICAL MEMORANDA.

COMPANY "C,"
73D REGIMENT ILLINOIS INFANTRY VOLUNTEERS.

BY W. H. NEWLIN.

ENLISTMENTS in the company dated from July 12, 1862, to April 11, 1864. One hundred and four names appear on the company roll. All members who enlisted on or before July 23, 1862, were sworn in, the first time, by John Newlin, J. P., in West's pasture, village of Georgetown, Vermillion County, Ill. On the same day, July 23d, Patterson McNutt, Mark D. Hawes, and Richard N. Davies, were elected captain, first and second lieutenants respectively.

July 24th, company transported in wagons from Georgetown to the "Y," a point on the T. W. & W. R. R., near the site of Tilton. Taking the cars at the "Y," company reached Camp Butler early next morning.

By August 1st company organization was completed, by appointment of the following named as sergeants: Tilmon D. Kyger, first sergeant; Wm. R. Lawrence, second sergeant; David A. Smith, third sergeant; Wm. H. Newlin, fourth sergeant; Robert B. Drake, fifth sergeant; and by the following named as corporals, in their order: David McDonald, John W. Smith, Carey A. Savage, Wm. M. Sheets, Samuel W. Sigler, Wm. O. Underwood, John V. Don Carlos, William Henderson. Pleasant B. Huffman, fifer; William B. Cowan, drummer; and Amacy M. Hasty, teamster.

Time, at Camp Butler, was spent in drilling, guarding prisoners, and other duty. Some pay and an installment of bounty was received by each member of the company. Twenty-five dollars bounty was paid by Vermillion County to each married man and ten dollars to each unmarried man. To hasten the muster in of regiment, Company C loaned to Company E—also enlisted in Vermillion County—fourteen men, all but three of whom were re-transferred to C. Regiment was mustered into United States service August 21, 1862.

August 24th, left camp Butler, going by rail via Danville, Ill., Lafayette Junction, Indianapolis, and Seymour, Ind., to Louisville, Ky. Went into quarters at Camp Jaquess—named for our colonel—south-west of the city. At this camp some guard duty was done, without arms, other than clubs and revolvers; all the clubs and nearly all the revolvers being soon discarded.

About August 30th regiment was supplied with muskets—Austrian or Belgium pattern—and ammunition for same. Muskets were of the *kicking* kind. From July 24th company had been in receipt of government rations, and was becoming inured to service in this respect.

September 1st or 2d moved to Camp Yates, three or four miles south-east of the city. Other regiments were at this camp, and a Division was formed, the Seventy-third and One Hundreth Illinois, and Seventy-ninth and Eigthy-eighth Indiana Regiments making one brigade, commanded by Colonel Kirk. Lieutenant Hawes and Sergeant Lawrence were detailed for duty at Kirk's head-quarters, and a very *ludricous* mistake was made, in *supposing* there were two vacancies created. Accordingly there was an advance along the line; Davies being promoted first lieutenant, as was thought; Orderly Kyger to second lieutenant; D. A. Smith to orderly, and Corporal John W. Smith to second sergeant, the latter being promoted over the writer. The joke fell heaviest on Kyger, as he incurred the expense of the purchase of sword, belt and straps. J. W. Smith resumed his place as corporal, much to the gratification of the writer, who did not like the idea of being "jumped."

Before the middle of September an inspection was ordered, requiring the command to march to Louisville, taking all luggage, accompanied also by wagon-train. The number and variety of articles thrown out of knapsacks and train was *amazing* to the *old* soldiers. This inspection was for the purpose of reducing luggage and baggage to articles of necessity. Directly after this the defeat of Union forces at Richmond, Ky., occurred. A rapid advance of a day's march was made by the command to assist in covering the retreat of those forces. Following this defeat came the invasion by Kirby Smith's Confederate forces, menacing Cincinnati and Covington. To meet this emergency the command was ordered at once to the latter place, going via Jeffersonville and Seymour, Ind., and Cincinnati, Ohio. The marching of the Seventy-third in the streets of Cincinnati excited comment, and inquiry was made if it was an old regiment. There was a fine engraving produced about this time representing the regiment, marching in column, on to the pontoon bridge.

Fears of invasion subsiding, the command was ordered back to Louisville, returning via Indianapolis. Buell's army having reached Louisville, a general reorganization of all forces—old and new—took place. The Forty-fourth and Seventy-third Illinois, and Second and Fifteenth Missouri Regiments formed the Thirty-fifth Brigade, Eleventh Division of reorganized army.

Bragg's army, which had followed Buell's into Kentucky, was gathering much strength and material in its march in the interior, and on October 1st the Union army was put in motion and started in pursuit. A dozen or more members of the company were left sick at Louisville. Army caught up with the enemy October 8th. Regiment was placed in and withdrawn from an exposed position, just in the "nick of time," a position within easy range of Confederate battery. Being withdrawn, as above, and resuming position in main line, regiment was actively engaged in battle of Perryville, nearly two hours, the casualties to Company C being as follows:

Josiah Cooper, wounded, ... Died Oct. 31, 1862.
Samuel Boen, wounded, ...
David W. Doop, wounded, ... Discharged Feb. 9, 1863.
John S. Long, wounded, ... Discharged Jan. 13, 1863, **died.**
Francis M. Stevens, wounded, ... Discharged Dec. 5, 1862.
Zimri Thornton, wounded, ... Died Oct. 30, 1862.
James E. Moore, wounded, ... Discharged March 17, 1863, lost foot.
John Murdock, Co. E, wounded, . . . Died, Oct. 9, 1862.

The last named enlisted in C, but had been one of the fourteen men "loaned," as before mentioned. Several members of

Company C, who had been left at Louisville, came up Oct. 9th and 10th.

Followed to Crab Orchard, marching from there, via Danville, Lebanon, Bowling Green, and Mitchellsville, to Nashville, Tenn. At Bowling Green, Rosecrans relieved Buell. Arrived at Nashville Nov. 7, 1862, encamping first at Edgefield, then at Mill Creek. Nov. 20, 1862, Second Lieutenant Richard N. Davies, resigned. Nov. 28th, First Lieutenant Mark D. Hawes resigned. These resignations, the losses resulting from the action at Perryville, the loss by death of the following named members: Samuel W. Blackburn, John C. Sheets, Thomas Millholland, Israel H. Morgan, John and Alex. Gerrard, and William Henderson; and the following named discharged for disability: Thos. T. Ashmore, John Trimble, and Wm. O. Underwood, discharged, Oct. 9, 1862, made a total loss to company by Jan. 1, 1863, of eighteen men. Three of these, viz: David W. Doop, John S. Long, and James E. Moore, were discharged after Jan. 1st, on Feb. 9th, Jan. 13th, and March 17th, 1863, respectively. Nov. 25, 1862, Kyger was mustered in as first lieutenant, and Dec. 6, 1862, Lawrence was mustered in as second lieutenant.

Dec. 26, 1862, started on movement to Stone River. Regiment not engaged until Dec. 31st, was then engaged fully one-third, and under fire two-thirds of the day. Seventy-third was in Second Brigade, of Sheridan's (Third) Division, Twentieth A. C., and associated with the same regiments as before. The change in number of Brigade and Division occurred when Rosecrans assumed command. At Stone River Company C suffered casualties as follows: John Dye and James Yoho, killed; John J. Halsted, wounded, discharged Feb. 23, 1863; three or four others very slightly wounded, and Lieutenant Lawrence and Daniel Suycott, captured. Lawrence and Suycott were exchanged in the following Spring, returning to the Company in May. About Jan. 7, 1863, a detail from company, Lieutenant Kyger in charge, sought the bodies of Dye and Yoho and buried them. The writer saw both these men expire; they were near together, and died at about the same time.*

---

* NOTE.—The latter part of January, or early in February, the company, in pursuance of general orders from Rosecrans, chose a man whose name

Were in two different camps at Murfreesboro, first Bradley, then Shafer—named for our brigade commander killed at Stone River. From Jan. 1st to June 30th, 1863, inclusive, the com-

should be inscribed on a "roll of honor." Through some unaccountable circumstance, or accident, or perhaps through compromise, the choice fell on the writer hereof. Though conscious of having tried to do my duty at Stone River, I knew this honor was undeserved; that there were others more entitled to it. As the honor was bestowed by comrades who had passed with me through the smoke and fire of that eventful day I will cherish it to my dying hour as a precious legacy, one that I would proudly transmit to my children if possible. Having mentioned the foregoing, I must not fail to record another scrap of history equally important in its outcome, as placing me under a weight of obligation to the company.

Some time in May, 1863, I was on picket duty as sergeant at outpost, from which guards were sent out every two hours to relieve those on the line. Guards at this outpost were expected to, and usually did, turn out and present arms to the officer of the day, or other officer, when he came around. On this particular day a cold, drizzling rain was falling, and the officer wore a gum coat, concealing insignia of office, or special duty. Four of the boys were pitching quoits (horse-shoes), as a means of diversion, when the officer on horseback was observed in the distance through woods. The quoit pitching ceased, and the boys made ready to "take arms" and "fall in." But the horseman either did not see, or pretended that he did not see the outpost, until he got well past a point in our front, then quickly turning, dashed upon us. As I was satisfied the officer was playing a "smart Aleck" game, I had said to the boys, "never mind; pay no attention to him," and only two or three turned out. Arriving at the outpost, reining his steed, and bowing up his neck with a self-satisfied air, as though he thought himself "autocrat of all the Russias," officer demanded, "Where's the corporal or sergeant in charge?" I responded "Here." Officer inquired my name, rank, and regiment. Noting the information I gave him, officer rode away, without giving his name, or business, as requested. The latter I learned next day on returning to camp. An order from Sheridan had been received by the company commander to "reduce Sergeant Wm. H. Newlin to the ranks; fill vacancy, etc." An investigation was had; those who had been on duty with me the past twenty-four hours and myself, were summoned, and all the facts were stated. The general's order was complied with—that had to be done—and an election was ordered to be held at nine o'clock next morning, to fill vacancy thus created. The hour for election arrived, and as there was no candidate against me I received a *unanimous* vote, and was elected—not appointed—to "fill vacancy." Division head-quarters was notified, "Order complied with; Wm. H. Newlin reduced, and vacancy filled." And that was the end of it, except that Lieutenant Kyger cautioned all the boys not to say any thing about the matter in writing home, adding, "What if news of that should get back to Georgetown?" But I did n't care where the news went to, whether to Georgetown or Damascus, so all the facts were given.

pany lost members as follows, in addition to the three already noted, viz:

John W. Smith,	. . . . . .	Discharged, Jan. 3, 1863, disability.
Carey A. Savage,	. . . . . .	Discharged, Feb. 6, 1863, disability.
John V. Don Carlos,	. . . .	Discharged, May 10, 1863, disability.
Enoch Braselton,	. . . . .	Discharged, March 12, 1863, disability.
William Cook,	. . . .	Discharged, Jan. 28, 1863, disability.
Robert W. Cowan,	. . . . .	Discharged, Feb. 9, 1863, disability.
Lawrence Dye,	. . . . . .	Discharged, Jan. 28, 1863, disability.
Benj. F. Edmonds,	. . . .	Discharged, Feb. 10, 1863, disability.
Wright Madden,	. . . . . .	Transferred to gun-boat service, April 16, 1863.
Jacob Martin,	. . . .	Died at Murfreesboro, Feb. 21, 1863.
William McEntyre,	. . . .	Died at Nashville, Jan. 15, 1863.
Thomas Elwood Madden,	.	Discharged, Feb. 20, 1863, disability.
Joshua T. Nicholson,	. . .	Died at Nashville, Jan. 18, 1863.
Christopher C. Shires,	. .	Discharged, May 28, 1863, disability.
John M. Thompson,	. . . .	Discharged, Feb. 20, 1863, disability.
James F. Williams,	. . . .	Discharged, March 26, 1863, disability.
George Miley,	. . . .	Died at Nashville, Feb. 3, 1863.
Robert B. Drake,	. . . . .	Discharged, June 30, 1863, disability.

In all, twenty-one men, making a total loss to July 1, 1863, of thirty-nine men.

Started June 23, 1863, on Chattanooga campaign. First injury to member of Company was the wounding of Alex. C. Nicholson, at Fairfield.

Followed on, passing Manchester and Estill Springs, wading Elk River, and passing through Winchester to Cowan's Station. Halted at latter place, July 3, 1863, hearing next day the news of Gettysburg and Vicksburg.

A few days later passed through Cumberland Tunnel, and on to Stevenson, Alabama. At Stevenson there was a delay until Sept. 2d, when the command pushed on to the Tennessee River, at Bridgeport, crossing on the 3d, and going over Sand Mountain, and on down to Alpine, Georgia. When company left Stevenson I remained, with others, in consequence of chills, having had medicine prescribed for breaking same about August 30th.

Captain Patterson McNutt resigned July 29, 1863, and First Lieutenant Tilmon D. Kyger was mustered in as captain of company, Sept. 4th, following.*

---

* NOTE.—On morning, Sept. 3d, we followed company to Bridgeport, arriving just as command was starting to cross the river. Being wearied by

The movement to Alpine, by Thomas' and McCook's corps, having forced Bragg out of Chattanooga, next came the hard marching necessary to concentrate the Union forces, before the reinforced enemy should turn and crush Crittenden's corps.

---

the tramp, James T. Maudlin, Henderson Goodwin, William Martin, and myself were again left in temporary hospital. Next morning, feeling much refreshed, concluded to apply for passes to go on to company. We were disappointed, myself in particular, as that date, Sept. 4, 1863, marked the end of my twenty-first year. About noon, a long wagon train began crossing the river, and while at dinner we conceived the idea of getting across, under the guise of train guards. So, striking the train at a little distance from the river, we distributed ourselves at intervals, among the wagons, loading our luggage, except gun and bayonet. The scheme worked; and on getting across, we repossessed ourselves of our luggage, and passed ahead of the train. We diligently pressed forward until sunset. We then located a camp, got roasting-ears from a field to our right, an iron pot, and water at a house to our left, and in due time feasted, chatted, and retired for the night, not knowing how near we might be to enemies, or how far from friends. After midnight a terrible racket, to our front, awakened and frightened us. Imagining the commotion was produced by a dash of the enemy's cavalry, we arose in great haste, scattered our fire, gathered our traps, and hied us away to the brush. The disturbance ceased, our excitement subsided, and we resumed our former position. After breakfast next morning we started, and on going one-fourth of a mile we came to a lot, of say three acres, in which were a dozen or more horses, colts, and cows. Up to nearly noon at least, we attributed the racket to the stock. Keeping steadily on, and not meeting or overtaking any troops or trains, and the road showing less indications of any having passed, we began to feel lonesome. Just before noon, after passing a house on our left, we stopped, and sent one of our squad back to inquire if any troops had passed that morning. Comrade soon returned with information that a small body of cavalry had passed, going south, about two hours before. Signs in the road, and on either side, seemed to confirm the report, but as our scout had failed to ascertain the character of the cavalry, he was sent for further information. In answer to question as to whose, or what cavalry had passed, our man was told it was "we'rn" Further inquiry established a probability that it was a detachment of Roddy's Confederate cavalry. For certain reasons we did not go back past the house, but kept straight ahead, as though it was our business to overtake that detachment. Fifteen minutes later we were following a road in an easterly direction. Going at a "quick" gait, and being about to pass a bunch of pigs, averaging about sixty pounds weight, we concluded we would n't pass all of them. It was very quickly done, as we dare not fire a gun, or allow a pig to squeal much. The choice parts of the pig were appropriated to our own special purposes. After dinner we pursued our way, and soon discovered intersecting roads, and evidences of the passage of troops and trains. Later our suspense was ended, and before dark, of Sept. 6th, we had reached the company.

Arrived in vicinity of Chickamauga battlefield, late September 18th. Got nearer next day; was under fire, but not engaged.

Saturday night, September 19th, company furnished a corporal, R. J. Hasty, and two or three guards for duty at Sheridan's head-quarters. McCook, Crittenden, and other generals, were at head-quarters in course of the night. Sheridan was restless and dissatisfied, and altogether indications, as interpreted by our corporal and guards, were unfavorable as to our prospects for to-morrow. Bradley's brigade (Sheridan's third), had been very roughly used in the afternoon, and his first and second brigades would probably "catch it" to-morrow. We were in the second (Laibold's brigade.) The night was dark, the weather was cool, and fire was forbidden. Our position was in heavy woods; the noise and racket in our front, whether made by the enemy or by our own troops, sounded and resounded terribly ominous in our ears. Daybreak came, and with it orders to move; we were out of rations, or nearly so, and not allowed time to draw a supply. Lytle persisted in drawing rations for his (the first) brigade, notwithstanding orders to move immediately. Moved two miles or more to the left; took position, and awaited further orders.

Before noon orders came, and we "went in." Of this memorable battle history tells; it has been "fought over," and "wrote up," many times. As within an hour from "going in," we had, with others, surrendered, and passed to the rear of five lines, two ranks each, of Confederate troops, we will not attempt a description of the small part of the battle we witnessed. For the first time we viewed the situation amid and to rear of the enemy. Doubt and uncertainty seemed to have place among the Confederates, although they were advancing. Officers were busy gathering up stragglers and hurrying them forward. Too many wanted to guard prisoners. Swords were drawn, and wildly flourished, and much ado made, probably because of the presence of so many "Yankees." Rope lines and traces, and other rope rigging to artillery, and sorghum stalks, sticking in haversacks of Bragg's men, attracted our attention. We saw Gen. Longstreet with an immense escort following him. We saw Gen. Hood lying under the fly of a tent, wounded; later he had his leg taken off. After one o'clock enemy's right fell back, and our left advanced. We saw several solid shot, skipping over the ground, which had been sent by Crittenden's batteries. We had many companions in our new and strange experience, and formed many new acquaintances, most of them of short duration. Some fourteen hundred of Gen. Sheridan's division, and many from other commands, had been collected in one place. Hesser and North, of Company A, and Brown and myself, of Company C, were one little squad of the Seventy-third that did not scatter much. We encountered no other members of our regiment until reaching Richmond.

Up to this point we have given facts, in the history of the company, of which we had personal knowledge. What few incidents or accidents in its history, from Chickamauga up to opening of Atlanta campaign here given are vouched for, my information touching the same being derived from reliable sources. The losses sustained by company in battle of Chickamauga were as follows: David A. Smith, Enoch Smith, and Artemas Terrell, killed; Wm. R. Lawrence, John R. Burk, Henderson Goodwin, Nathaniel Henderson, Henry C. Henderson, Austin Henderson, Jehu Lewis (color bearer), and John Bostwick (discharged May 27, 1864), wounded; and all the following named were captured, viz: Enoch P. Brown, Wm. H. Newlin, John R. Burk, Wm. F. Ellis, Austin Henderson, and John Thornton. Of those that were captured, Burk and Lewis were soon exchanged, being seriously wounded; Burk, however, went to Richmond; losing an arm, he was discharged June 9, 1864. Lewis was exchanged on battlefield. Austin Henderson was exchanged late in 1864. John Thornton, Enoch P. Brown, and William F. Ellis, died in Andersonville prison, in order named: September 16th, 20th, and 23d, 1864, respectively. Number of Brown's grave, 9,350; Ellis', 9,703. Number of Thornton's grave not given. Wm. H. Newlin was never either paroled or exchanged. Nearly every member of company was struck by balls, or fragments of shell, or trees, in some part of the body, accoutrements, or clothing. At nightfall only three of the company were present at call of the captain. During the night a dozen or more others rallied upon this feeble remnant. Chickamauga was a dreadful strain upon the strength and powers of endurance of the soldier, and September 20, 1863, is, and will ever be, a memorable day in our country's history. By September 22d, some twenty or more of the company had reached Chattanooga, and were beginning to assume at least a defensive attitude. Early in September commissions for Lawrence and Smith, as first and second lieutenants, respectively, were sent for, but neither were ever mustered in on them; Lawrence resigning, November 24, 1863, as second lieutenant, and Smith having met his fate as already noted.

Following Chickamauga came the siege of Chattanooga, and with it very scant supplies, and hard picket and forage duty. The "cracker line" being often disturbed, and foraging not yielding, or "panning out" very heavily, the supply of rations, provender, for man and beast, was far short of ordinary demands. November 25th the battle of Missionary Ridge occurred, in which Company C fortunately suffered very few casualties, the most serious one being the wounding of Stephen Newlin. After Missionary Ridge company and command went to the relief of Burnside at Knoxville. On this winter campaign much hard marching and great fatigue were endured. Some one or two, or more, of the company, not starting with the command, followed up later with squads and detachments. In one or more instances the enemy's cavalry attempted to "gobble up" these squads. During its stay in East Tennessee, regiment encamped for a time at Haworth's Mill, near New Market, and also at Lenoir's Station. From latter place, it is said, some members of company made frequent visits in the country east of river, and it is further alleged, one or more of them got married. Dandridge, I believe, was the farthest point eastward to which command penetrated in the Knoxville campaign. Capt. Kyger was very sick at Knoxville, in course of winter, and on recovering sufficiently was granted leave of absence.

Winter breaking, and time for opening of the Atlanta campaign approaching, the regiment returned to vicinity of Chattanooga, encamping at Cleveland, at which point we rejoined it, on our return from prison. April 11, 1864, Wm. R. Cook was mustered in, as a recruit to company, being last name entered on company roll.*

From June 30, 1863, to July 1, 1864, the total loss to company, from all causes, was fourteen men, including Amos Bogue. Transferred to Invalid corps, August 1, 1863; Clark B. Brant,

---

* NOTE.—Soon after capture were placed under a strong guard, our partners, being Brown, Hesser, and North. Jos. C. Squires, an attachee, before capture, of Gen. Rosecrans' staff, "stood in" with us a day or so, until catching sight of Col. Von Strader. We dropped our extra ammunition in Chickamauga Creek. Passed Ringgold, Sunday evening, about eight o'clock. Four miles farther on, halted until morning. Arrived at Tunnell Hill about noon, September 21st. A morsel of bacon issued to each man, a piece four inches long, could have been drawn through a half-inch augur hole, without squeezing out much grease. Boarded railroad train about three o'clock, P. M., and started on tour of Confederacy. Rode on top of car part of time; came near rolling off. Reached Atlanta night of September 22d. Put up at Barracks. Next day were marched past a clerk at a table; gave clerk our name, company and regiment. Drew rations, September 24th. Started early; arrived at Augusta before night. Bought a huge watermelon; all we could do to carry it; cost fifty cents. Were guarded closely in court-house enclosure. Got away with melon by calling neighbors. September 25th, took an early train for Columbia. Cars crowded as usual; excitement subsiding; novelty of trip wearing off. Reached Columbia morning of 26th. Were delayed three hours. Finally got started northward, the direction we wanted to go, if we did n't stop too soon. Rode all day up to three o'clock. Stopped at a little station near line between the Carolinas. Lots of sweet potatoes on the platform; we let them alone. Many people were there, mostly women, young and old. An old lady delivered an off-hand address, giving advice to the "Yankees." She wanted to know why we "could n't let the South alone. We're not meddlin' with your affairs. You all go back North and stay on your farms, and in your factories, and work-shops. Yes, go back to your homes and make shoes for us." Reached Charlotte late in the day. A few of the boys got away, and trouble and delay were occasioned in getting them to train again. Next day, Sunday, September 27th, arrived at Raleigh. Were viewed by many people, mostly colored, while waiting. Got under way again, traveled all night, arriving at Weldon next day. Dismounted from cars; were guarded near railroad; drew rations. Invested one dollar and a half in extras. Boarded train early on September 29th, and dismounted no more until arriving at Richmond. Put up at Libby about eleven o'clock the night of 29th. Paid Dick Turner twelve dollars next day under protest. He said he would pay it back when we were paroled or exchanged. Was never paroled or exchanged, so the twelve dollars ain't due yet. Went to the Rosser (tobacco) house late on the 30th. We were guided around to it. Stayed one night with Rosser, then went to Smith and Pemberton houses, October 1st. On the way fell in with Ellis and Thornton, of Company C. Stationary for quite a while; had a diversity of pastime, read Testament, played checkers, fought vermin,

discharged November 12, 1863; Merida Thornton and Aaron Willison, transferred to Invalid corps, January 15th and February 1, 1864; James T. Slaughter, transferred to V. R. C., May 1, 1864; Charles W. Cook, permanently detached as blacksmith to Bat. G., First Mo. Art., August 26, 1863; and James

but never carried any rations over from one day to next. Kilpatrick— Jesse D., not James, as we have it on page 10—joined our Seventy-third delegation; his credentials were from Company B. Got our share of the sugar. Stopped one night at Scott House; next day, November 14th, took train for Danville, Va., arriving November 15th. Our delegation generally agreed, worked and voted as a unit on all questions. Consisting of seven members, we settled things among ourselves in committee, before going to the full house. Attention was occupied a few days considering a plan for a general break; plan never fully matured, i. e. in the full house; killed in committee, no doubt. December 15th we seceded, withdrew from prison No. 2, on account of small-pox, and went to hospital. In time recovered, and was variously employed up to February 19, 1864. Formed new acquaintances; organized a new alliance; seceded again, the night of date last mentioned.

In issue of *National Tribune* of November 16, 1882, my comrade L. B. Smith, criticises my narrative, in a manner complimentary to it, however. He says, "Many important points are left out; all he has written is true, and much more." Have supplied one of those "important points" on page 4, the very *important* one to comrade Smith. I refer to his rescue, by Sutherland, from drowning in Craig's Creek. Another interesting, if not "important point," left out, is that which includes the proposal, from a mulatto girl of some fifteen Summers, that we should leave Smith with herself and parents as a "hostage," security that we, after getting through, would send a squad of cavalry after the whole family. Other interesting points were some of our disenssions as to feasibility of things proposed, such as the taking of the horses, the third night out; which road to take—this, that, or the other; and the project of unearthing money said to be hid in a certain portion of a river bank. Another important and interesting point in Mr. Smith's life did not come within the compass of my narrative, viz.: his standing guard for a few minutes over Mr. Jefferson Davis, immediately after, or within a day or two of his capture. Mr. Smith became twenty-one years old in February, 1864, while on our trip. The cut—upper left corner—represents Smith as he appeared at about the age of thirty years. Another interesting point was the management, making a friend, by Sutherland, of Huffman's dog. So skillfully did Sutherland get on the "good side" of the dog that he never barked once, or gave his owner the slightest intimation or warning of our approach. Comrade Sutherland, I believe, was connected, in or about, the despatching of Maj. Ross' dog in Richmond. Mr. Sutherland is, and has always been a farmer; is now fifty years old; cut— lower right corner—represents him as he appeared probably ten years ago. Other interesting points left out are those in the experience of comrade Tripp, after his separation from our party, March 4, 1864. Did not know

W. Trimble, transferred to V. R. C., April 10, 1864, the other seven already noted; making a total loss to date of fifty-three men.

Moved from Cleveland, May 3, 1864, with command, first brigade, second division, fourth army corps. Under fire first time, on Atlanta campaign, in the vicinity of Catoosa Springs, May 5. At Rocky Faced Ridge, May 9th, was again under fire, but not engaged. Sharpshooters from the regiment did good work here; Company C being represented by John P.

---

until November, 1881, that Tripp had survived these experiences. Visiting him last November I learned the particulars of his singular and somewhat protracted wanderings after we left him. Want of space forbids any thing like a record of them here. His loneliness, immediately following his misfortune in being left, must have been oppressive; hungry and foodless, the shades of night closing around him amid those rugged mountains, his feelings can scarcely be imagined. With reluctance and fear he called, hoping his recent companions, or some belated pursuer, might hear him; but there was no answering voice, nothing but distressing silence, and his disappointment was very great. Mr. Tripp is now fifty-seven years old; cut—lower left corner—shows him as he appeared for some months after his discharge in December, 1864. Wood and Taylor are accounted for on page 4. In Wood's case the information is direct and official; he was about twenty-six years old at time of his death. In Taylor's case the information is indirect and circumstantial, but his fate is probably correctly indicated on page 4. He was about twenty-seven years old at time we left him.

The engravings herewith, "The Ferry Scene," and "Left Alone," are reasonably accurate and true to the reality. "Out of the Woods" is intended to represent the general idea of escape, our troubles behind, our persevering, unremitting efforts ended, and our safety assured. Though as uniting, bringing together, two or three separate scenes, "Out of the Woods" is also a faithful picture. Conceding that Taylor's fate, as the principal figure in "Left Alone," was that, which all the information suggests, indescribably sad, and gloomy must have been his last hour. Nothing of hope or comfort in his anticipations of the future, his busy thoughts must have drifted away from his surroundings and recent events, and sped across the sea, and dwelt upon his father and mother there, who were ignorant of his fate. This brings us to the events mentioned on page 109. At Georgetown, while on furlough, we met Capt. Kyger and P. B. Huffman, of Company C. Furlough soon run out. The rocks and hills about Georgetown seemed very small. Separated from home and friends once more, and started in company with Huffman for the front. This was in the latter part of April. Encountered my escaping comrade Sutherland in Indianapolis, and accompanied him the greater part of the way to Chattanooga. Arrived in camp at Cleveland, May 2, 1864, just at sunset. Had to talk nearly all night, and then get up next morning and start on the Atlanta campaign.

Jones, Alex. C. Nicholson, and James T. Maudlin. Was engaged at Resaca, May 14th. Wm. D. Bales struck by piece of shell. Was engaged at Adairsville, May 17th. Up to, and including Adairsville, Company C was in my charge, there being no commissioned officer present. On this date Capt. Kyger arrived at the front and took command of company. At Kingston there was a delay of three or four days. Pursuant to orders, all vacancies in line, and non-commissioned officers were filled, or selections made with that object in view. May 22d, Company C attended to this duty. The company was entitled to a lieutenant, and an election was held. Candidates were voted for, for orderly sergeant, with the understanding that the successful candidate should be commissioned first lieutenant. Election resulted in my favor by a small majority—four votes, I believe—which, considering all the circumstances, my long absence, and the fact that my competitor had been present all the time, was a No. 1 soldier, none better, I regarded as extremely flattering, and was therefore very thankful for the advancement.

My commission was sent for; it bears date June 9, 1864. The list of non-commissioned officers being filled, stood as follows:

Wm. M. Sheets, orderly sergeant.
James T. Maudlin, second sergeant.
Jehu Lewis, third sergeant.
Robert J. Hasty, fourth sergeant.
Alex. C. Nicholson, fifth sergeant.
Wesley Bishop, first corporal.
Jonathan Ellis, second corporal.
Austin Henderson, third corporal.
Samuel Hewitt, fourth corporal.
Alfred E. Lewis, fifth corporal.
George W. Martin, sixth corporal.
Stephen Newlin, seventh corporal.
Geo. Hollingsworth, eighth corporal.

It was at this time and place that A. E. Lewis notified Ellis of his appointment as corporal; adding, "and your commission has gone on to Washington for approval." All of the above were mustered out June 12, 1865. The list does not contain one of the original sergeants or corporals; except that Orderly Sheets was one of the first corporals.

Recommenced active operations about May 25th. June 18th John Braselton was wounded. By June 25th the actions at Pine and Lost Mountains, Dallas, New Hope Church, and preliminary battles before Kenesaw Mountain had taken place, without inflicting serious damage to company. Capt. Kyger was sick, a week or more, up to and including June 27th, the day of the assault on Kenesaw. This assault was the first heavy battle occurring after my muster in as lieutenant, and owing to the formation of each regiment preparatory to the assault, and the absence of my seniors, I was placed in command of two companies, C and H, forming the third or middle division of regiment. Two lines, of two ranks each, were in front of, and two lines, of two ranks each, were in rear of companies C and H. Owing to nature of ground these companies came off well, suffered less than any of the others. From point of starting in, the ground sloped considerably to line immediately without, or in front of the very elaborate, systematic obstructions in front of enemy's works, and from this same line the ground covered by these obstructions was gradually ascending to line of fortifications. Pending the heaviest fire of enemy, companies C and H were on the lowest ground, all the other companies, whether in front or rear, being on higher ground, so that fire of enemy was comparatively harmless to C and H, there being only four or five slight wounds received in the two companies, and these inflicted while getting back to position from which they started. Of the regiment, three were killed, and some twelve or fifteen wounded. There were several cases of overheating, the weather being extremely hot, and the assault, from some cause, not being made as early as intended. The casualties to regiment, seeming so few, in an assault of such magnitude, it is proper to state that number of men in regiment that day, present for duty, did not exceed three hundred. In our front, too, were very heavy earth-works, feebly manned; but for the arrival of reinforcements we could have effected, at least, a *temporary* breach in the enemy's line.

Early July 3d it was found that the enemy had fallen back. Followed up immediately; regiment lost one man, killed, July 4th. There was a delay of a week at the Chattahoochie River. Command took position, near river, above Vining's Station. July 9th division marched to Roswell; destroyed some mills or factories, and crossed and recrossed the Chattahoochie while gone, returning on the 12th. Writer was not with company on Roswell trip; but owing to depletion of strength was favored;

left behind in charge of regimental camp, and those who had been excused from duty. July 13th, crossed Chattahoochie River on pontoon bridge. While crossing, writer was taken sick, and was obliged to drop behind soon after getting across the river. In attempting to reach the upland and overtake company, was prostrated, the result of over-heating or partial sun-stroke, and have no recollection whatever of events occurring after the crossing of the Chattahoochie, up to the crossing of Nance's Creek, July 18. There had, however, been a delay at Buck's Head, and also a general inspection. Late on the 19th there were two or three severe skirmishes along the line of Peach Tree Creek, one of which approached the dignity of a battle, and several prisoners, including a general officer, were captured by our forces. Crossed Peach Tree Creek at ten o'clock, P. M., of the 19th.

About noon, on the 20th, brigade was assigned position in line, and hastily built slight breast-works of logs, limbs, and rails. This done, was ordered to make reconnoisance to front. In execution of this order, the enemy was found in force, and we came back at a double-quick, to find our temporary works occupied by other troops. Took another position, further to right, the Seventy-third holding the extreme right of fourth corps. There was a gap of two hundred yards or more, between right of fourth and left of twentieth corps; so the right of Seventy-third was retired, swung back a little in order to cover this gap. The battle immediately opened, giving no time for construction of works, however slight, and continued about an hour, with two casualties to Company C—William Martin and the writer, wounded. Sampson McCool, of Company E, was also wounded. Sampson and William McCool, and John Murdock, the latter killed at Perryville, being the three loaned by Company C to Company E, that were never retransferred to C. Of regiment, one man was killed, and several others wounded. My wound, being slight, healed entirely by August 1st, but I was detained at division field hospital until August 16th, on account of general physical debility, resulting from the sunstroke of 13th. Command was not in the battles of July 22d and 28th, so my hospital and prison experience, covering in all eight months, deprived me of participation in only one battle—Missionary Ridge—and one campaign—the East Tennessee—in which the company engaged.

The latter part of August, started on the flanking movement to Jonesboro and Lovejoy station. September 1st, engaged in tearing up railroad, burning the ties, and twisting the heated rails around trees. Arrived at Jonesboro too late to accomplish more than the capture of a hospital and a few hundred prisoners, as the battle there was closing. Night of September 1st, Company C stood picket out north-east of Jonesboro, and toward morning the rumble of Hood's artillery and trains could be heard, as they were passing hurriedly on a road still further eastward, retreating from Atlanta. Later, the explosions at Atlanta were distinctly heard. Followed on to Lovejoy's. Were under fire, but had no good opportunity of returning it. Withdrew from enemy's front at Lovejoy's the night of September 5th or 6th, returning to Atlanta, arriving on the 8th. Went into quarters with some expectation of remaining inactive for a longer time than we did. Writer, however, saw the exterior of the barracks, the interior of which he had seen, as a prisoner, just a year before.

About September 26th to 28th, were ordered to Chattanooga, going by railway; and from thence marched down into Alpine valley again, about October 18th, returning the latter part of October, via Chickamauga battle-ground, to Chattanooga. On this return march from Alpine, quite a number of recruits of Fifty-first Illinois fell behind, "straggled," and no wonder, as most of them wore overcoats, and carried knapsacks packed full; one of them carried his bayonet fixed, instead of in scabbard, whereupon Corporal Lewis (who had just awakened from a short sleep at roadside, where company was resting) cried out, "Halt, halt, you Fifty-firster; I want to know WHERE YOU GOT YOUR GUN SHARPENED."

About November 1, 1864, went by rail to Huntsville, Alabama, and from there marched to Athens, and from thence, via Lynnville and Pulaski, to Columbia, Tenn. Here a part of twenty-third corps met, and reinforced the fourth corps. Hood's rebel army was becoming very troublesome and apparently impatient for large results, and was pressing ours very *closely*. Considerable skirmishing took place about Columbia, in which Company C bore its full share. Under pressure of enemy our forces crossed Duck River the night of November 28th, the Seventy-third standing picket the balance of that night on north bank of river. Next morning, the pressure being great, there was no time to relieve us, and being already deployed, we fell back, first as flankers, then as skirmishers, in the direction of Spring Hill, arriving there about four o'clock in afternoon of 29th. We were to the right, or south-east of Pike and of Spring Hill. The part of the Seventy-third in the action at Spring Hill was to assist in resisting a cavalry dash by enemy, just before sunset. To do this we were only compelled to shorten our line a little, and deliver a brisk fire for the space of about ten minutes. Heavy fighting was going on near us, in which enemy's infantry was engaged, pending which, night fall ended the contest, luckily for our forces. There was great confusion, one result of which was, our being compelled to stand picket all night, as on the preceding night. We must have been VERY CLOSE indeed to enemy's pickets, though we did not see or hear them; but could distinctly see the enemy at a little distance around his camp-fires. Our trains were hustling the whole night through, and got well on the way before morning toward Franklin.

Daylight of November 30th came, and we were still on the picket line. By sunrise we began falling back, deployed as skirmishers, and skirmishing began, and was kept up with more or less severity to within one mile of Franklin, when our brigade was relieved. Very soon after skirmishing began in the morning we crossed to the left of the road, and when but little more than half way to Franklin, Capt. Kyger being sick, was unable to remain longer with company, and was taken in charge by Surgeon Pond, and we saw him no more until arriving at Nashville. Being relieved, as before mentioned, by passing within, and to rear, of skirmish line, which had been thrown out, the brigade, Opedycke's first brigade, second division, fourth army corps, formed and marched in column, with little delay, to Franklin, passing on the way a brigade which must have been the third brigade of our division, posted some distance in front of a temporary line of breastworks, which had been hastily built, extending from a point above to another point on the river below the town. These works, scarcely a mile in length, semi-circular in form, and covering, not only Franklin, but also the bridge across the Harpeth, were filled with troops; so our brigade passed on to the rear, and took position behind Carter's Hill. This was at about 3:30 o'clock, P. M. The men at once set about preparing coffee and something to eat, being greatly fatigued from loss of sleep, and almost constant duty since evening of 28th, on crossing Duck River. All the trains, and the first division of the fourth corps, were north of the Harpeth.

Dinner over once, we should probably have followed and taken the advance, having assisted two days in covering the retreat. But no; not all of us were permitted to finish dinner before Hood had martialed his forces, swept up suddenly, driving in the brigade, posted in front, as before stated, in its wake, and under cover of same crushing in, making a fearful breach in our main line. Heavy firing began, clouds of dust and smoke arose, hundreds of rebel troops were thrust into the breach which they had made, and beyond; singly, and in squads, small and great, our men began flying from the front, throwing away their guns; pieces of artillery and cassions, with horses attached, came thundering down; confusion and consternation indescribable had been wrought in five minutes or less time.

The Thirty-sixth, Forty-fourth, and Seventy-third Illinois, and Twenty-fourth Wisconsin, and One Hundred and Twenty-fifth Ohio, five regiments, composing Opedycke's brigade, were instantly on their feet, anticipating orders, seizing their guns, which had been stacked on one line, made a simultaneous, irresistible rush to the front, carrying every thing before them at the point of the bayonet, capturing thirteen battle-flags, nearly one thousand prisoners, and restoring and strengthening our line, so that it was broken no more. Stung to desperation at this sudden turning of the scales in this important battle, the infuriated enemy *charged*, and CHARGED *again* and AGAIN, carrying his reckless resistance right up to, yes on to, our slight works, to the very muzzles of our guns. But we were there to stay, at least until getting ready to leave of our own accord; but it took *work*, HARD WORK, PERSISTENT, UNFLAGGING and UNFLINCHING WORK, to maintain our position. How it was done I can scarcely hope to describe.

On arriving at the point from whence our forces had been driven, there were too many troops to operate to advantage, and afford all a semblance of protection. Fortunately, the ground, beginning at the works, was gradually declining to the rear. Company C, with a few soldiers of other companies, was posted between, and to the front of, two pieces of artillery. All were either lying on the ground or in a low, stooping posture. Immediately at the works was a strong line of men, with barely elbow room, who did nothing but fire; in rear, of this line were two or three tiers of men, who were busy loading pieces and passing them forward; to rear of these were still others, who were cleaning guns, breaking open boxes of ammunition, and distributing cartridges to the loaders; others still further back, carried up the boxes of ammunition from a point where left by ammunition wagons. There was *work* for all, and all WORKED. There was a full half hour of desperate fighting, perhaps equalled at some time and place, but scarcely ever, if ever, surpassed. For several fearful minutes, as a result of combined, sturdy, heroic effort on the part of all, from end to end of our line, the small arms volleyed; there was no determining of intervals between volleys; it was as one. The cannon thundered; the shell shrieked; the smoke rolled; the earth trembled; the heroic, reckless, desperate, enemy surged, and *surged* again and AGAIN, right up to our line, and recoiled as often, *recoiling last*, before the merciless tempest of death.

Darkness came on, and shrouded the scene; there was a lull in the fight; a great calm after a great storm. Many of our soldiers had been slain, but for each one, from three to five of the rebels had bitten the dust. Very many on both sides were wounded, the few mortally, the many slightly. Did those who had not finished dinner, now finish it? No. Was supper prepared? No. Was there time for coffee? Not much. The foe, threatening and defiant, was right there, within sixty feet, waiting to pounce upon us. Guns were put in order, ammunition in abundance was got ready at hand, and all precautions taken. Nor had we long to wait until the first night assault was made; right up to our works they charged, coming within space measured by the flashes from our rifles. But before our galling fire the enemy quailed and fell back. Our fire slackened some; but within an hour two or more assaults were made, with like result.

After the last assault we kept up a heavy fire for some minutes, until some person, some officer perhaps, between the lines, but nearest ours, yelled out: "Cease firing, cease firing;" repeating the command several times. Amid the smoke and darkness it could not be told who or what he was, whether Union or rebel. In a few minutes the firing did, in a great measure, cease; later it ceased almost entirely. At same time a burning building in the suburbs of Franklin fell in, making a great light, by which we saw several, as many as a dozen, standards raise along enemy's line. He was preparing, no doubt, for a last desperate effort to break our front. Brisk firing immediately opened from our side, increasing in volume and ceasing not until every battle-flag on enemy's front was laid low. This ended the contest; quiet succeeded; and by midnight our weary forces had withdrawn from the field; crossed the Harpeth, and were slowly wending their way to Nashville.

The loss to Seventy-third, in this battle, was nine killed and two wounded that died soon afterward; one of the former being Adjt. Wilmer, and one of the latter being Major Motherspaw; the loss to Company C being one killed, Zenas Fulton, and one wounded, Joseph A. Allison, who died in enemy's hands. There were three or four others of company wounded, including the writer; and there were several others of the regiment wounded; but nearly all of these were slight wounds, excepting that of Captain Jonas Jones, and one or two others. Some two or three years ago writer saw a statement from Gen. D. S. Stanley, who commanded the fourth corps, until wounded, in this battle; which statement, published in a Philadelphia paper, asserted that the fourth corps used ninety wagon loads of ammunition the afternoon and night of November 30, 1864. It is reasonable to suppose that much of this ammunition was destroyed; wasted in other ways than in "wild firing," the enemy's losses, al told, being about five thousand five hundred, or three times our own.

Col. Opedycke was breveted brigadier-general, and merited praise was bestowed in congratulatory orders, for the part borne by his brigade in the battle of Franklin. Any other brigade that was there would probably have done as well, under the same circumstances; but as three-fifths of the brigade were Illinoisians we take a pardonable pride in making this imperfect record of its most conspicuous achievement.

Arrived at Nashville at one o'clock, P. M., December 1, 1864. We were a very tired, sorely-taxed, and dirty lot of soldiers. Sleep was imperatively demanded; and most of us, as soon as halted, or assigned camping space, dropped on the ground and slept until sunset; by which time Capt. Kyger had found us, and was anxiously ascertaining how we had fared. Hood followed up immediately, taking position in our front; and on December 3d, James Ashmore, of Company C; a faithful soldier, was shot dead while standing picket. His body was buried in the cemetery at Nashville. This was the last loss which befell Company C, except in case of two or three members who were mustered out a few days in advance of the regiment at hospitals, and one recruit—Wm. R. Cook—transferred to the Forty-fourth Illinois. About this time we received notification of the death of three members of the company in Andersonville prison, as before noted, viz.: Brown, Ellis, and Thornton, with whom the writer had spent three months as a prisoner. How fortunate had we been, not only in escaping prison, but in passing comparatively unharmed through twelve battles, since separating from prison comrades, and standing now upon the threshold of the thirteenth, destined to pass safely through that. Fortunate indeed we were, and thankful, very thankful we are, and ought to be.

On December 15th and 16th, 1864, occurred the battles of Nashville, in which command performed the part assigned it both days; in the afternoon of the 16th joining in the grand, majestic charge, which was the finishing stroke to the rebellion in the west. Casualties to Company C, none to speak of, and to regiment very few, only one man killed, and probably a dozen wounded. Enemy hugged his works so closely that his fire passed above our heads. On our reaching the works, those of the enemy who did not surrender fled with precipitated haste. With utmost enthusiasm our troops pursued the flying enemy, until darkness closed the race. Started early on the 17th, but our cavalry took the job off our hands, pursuing Hood so closely that he crossed the Tennessee River, with only a few shattered and broken fragments of his late offensive army. We followed to Pulaski, Tenn., at which point, a day or two before Christmas, we heard, for the last time, the whiz of an enemy's bullet.

Leaving Pulaski we took up our line of march for Huntsville, Ala., arriving January 5, 1865. Here we remained until March 28th; then going by rail to Blue Springs, East Tennessee. While at Blue Springs the war closed; Lee and Johnston surrendered, and Abraham Lincoln was assassinated. News of the latter produced the wildest frenzy among our troops. The latter part of April were ordered to Nashville. Going by rail, we arrived in due course. Hostilities having ceased, the excitement incident thereto having subsided, we led a quiet camp life up to middle of June. The regiment was mustered out June 12, 1865, starting a day or two later for Springfield, Ill., to receive final payment and to disband.

We give name of each member of Company C that was present for muster out June 12th, except where already noted; see list of sergeants and corporals and remarks below on page 126, which with the fifty-three men dropped from the roll by July 1, 1864, and the following dropped since, or mustered out in advance of the regiment, make the one hundred and four men, with which company entered the service: N. Brady and I. W. Ward, transferred to United States engineer corps, July 20th and August 21st, 1864; E. P. Brown, Wm. F. Ellis, and John Thornton, died at Andersonville; James A. Allison and Zenas Fulton, killed at Franklin; James Ashmore, killed at Nashville; Nathaniel Henderson, mustered out May 4th; William B. Cowan, May 17th, John Braselton, June 2d, and Daniel Suycott, June 8, 1865; Samuel W. Sigler, transferred to Veteran Reserve Corps, January 10, 1865, and William R. Cook, transferred to Forty-fourth Illinois, June 12, 1865, fourteen in all.

TILMON D. KYGER, deceased.	JOHN P. JONES.
WILLIAM H. NEWLIN.	THOMAS JUDD.
DAVID McDONALD.	ABRAHAM JONES.
PLEASANT B. HUFFMAN,	CLAIBORNE MADDEN.
SAMUEL J. BOEN.	WILLIAM MARTIN.
DAVID BRANSON,* deceased.	JAMES S. PECK, deceased.
WILLIAM D. BALES.	HARLAND H. REAGON.
JOHN DOOP.	JOSEPH W. REAGON.
HENDERSON GOODWIN.	WALTER SCOTT.
AMACY M. HASTY.	ISAAC H. THOMPSON.*
HENRY C. HENDERSON.	BENJAMIN PURDUM.
GEORGE J. HARRIER.	ISAAC R. THORNTON.

In all, ... 24
Add five sergeants and eight corporals, ... 13
Previously dropped from all causes as indicated, ... 67

Total, ... 104

DANVILLE, ILL., September 4, 1886.

---

*On detached service in rear, full term.

"January 1, 1861, the army of the United States for active service consisted of 14,663 men. May 1, 1865, there were 797,807 men on active duty, while 202,709 more were absent. During the struggle there were 44,000 killed in battle, 186,000 died from disease, 26,000 died in rebel prisons, 49,000 died from wounds, 280,000 were wounded, and 185,000 recorded captured and missing."

The above is quoted from the *Hand-book of Battles in the War of the Rebellion*, issued in 1887 by the Illinois Central Railroad Company, A. H. Hanson, General Passenger Agent, and dedicated to the

Grand Army of the Republic.

From the same source we glean the following statistics: "The first Confederates captured by Union forces was on May 10, 1861, at Camp Jackson, Mo. Number captured, 639. The first Federals captured by rebel forces was on July 21, 1861, at Manassas, or Bull Run, Va. Number missing and captured, 1,460. The largest number of Confederates falling at any one time into Federal hands was on July 4, 1863, at Vicksburg, Miss. Number of prisoners, 31,600. The largest number of Federals falling at any one time into Confederate hands was at Shiloh, or Pittsburg Landing, Tenn., April 6 and 7, 1862. Number of prisoners, 3,956."

We give these figures as reported by the authority quoted from, which omits any mention of Vicksburg, and we had to consult "Grant's Memoirs" to ascertain the number of Confederates surrendered at that point July 4, 1863. Probably the greatest number of Federals falling at any one time, or within a brief period, into Confederate hands was during the seven days' retreat of the Army of the Potomac, June 26 to July 1, 1862, in which the number of Federals *missing* is reported by "Hand-book" at 13,399. The Federal prisoners taken at Chickamauga are embraced under the general head of *missing*—number, 4,945. The greatest number of Confederates reported as *missing* in any one engagement is 13,621, July 1 to 3, 1863, at Gettysburg.

There seems to be no data or statistics whatever showing the number of Federal prisoners who attempted an escape from captivity, or showing what percentage of those attempting or starting on a trip of that kind succeeded in their efforts. The first record made, probably, in cases of success in this line was when individual prisoners or small squads first reported within the Federal lines; and in cases of failure, the data or record, if any, was made by Confederate authority.

NOTE.—We have never been able to fully verify the record of the unfortunate comrade, Taylor, mentioned on page 53 of this narrative. A mystery surrounds his fate. Why he persisted in being "left alone" is a question we can not answer. He may, for some reason, have misled us by giving a wrong given name at the time we left him. We had learned, become familiar with his surname, and also the name and number of the regiment he belonged to, before any motive could have existed in his mind to prompt him to deceive us. We have relinquished the task of further verifying his record.

STUDY THIS ADVERTISEMENT,

Drs. STARKEY & PALEN'S
Treatment by Inhalation.

1529 Arch Street, Philad'a, Pa.

— FOR —

Consumption, Asthma, Bronchitis, Dyspepsia, Catarrh, Hay Fever, Headache, Debility, Rheumatism, Neuralgia,

— AND —

→※ ALL CHRONIC AND NERVOUS DISORDERS. ※←

"The Compound Oxygen Treatment," Drs. Starkey & Palen, No 1529 Arch Street, Philadelphia, have been using for the last seventeen years, is a scientific adjustment of the elements of Oxygen and Nitrogen, *magnetized*, and the compound is so condensed and made portable that it is sent all over the world.

DRS. STARKEY & PALEN have the liberty to refer to the following-named well-known persons who have tried their treatment:

HON. WM. D. KELLEY, Member of Congress, Philadelphia.
REV. VICTOR L. CONRAD, Editor Lutheran Observer, Philadelphia.
REV. CHARLES W. CUSHING, D. D., Rochester, N. Y.
HON. WM. PENN NIXON, Editor Inter-Ocean, Chicago, Ill.
W. H. WORTHINGTON, Editor New South, Birmingham, Ala.
JUDGE H. P. VROOMAN, Quenemo, Kansas.
MRS. MARY A. LIVERMORE, Melrose, Massachusetts.
JUDGE R. S. VOORHEES, New York City.
MR. E. C. KNIGHT, Philadelphia.
M. FRANK SIDDALL, Merchant, Philadelphia.
HON. W. W. SCHUYLER, Easton, Penn.
EDWARD L. WILSON, 833 Broadway, N. Y., Ed. Phila. Photo.
FIDELIA M. LYON, Waimea, Hawaii, Sandwich Islands.
ALEXANDER RITCHIE, Inverness, Scotland.
MRS. MANUEL V. ORTEGA, Fresnillo, Zacatecas, Mexico.
MRS. EMMA COOPER, Utilla, Spanish Honduras, C. A.
J. COBB, Ex-vice Consul, Casablanca, Morocco.
M. V. ASHBROOK, Red Bluff, Cal.
JAMES MOORE, Sup't Police, Blandford, Dorsetshire, England.
JACOB WARD, Bowral, New South Wales.

And thousands of others in every part of the United States.

"*Compound Oxygen: Its Mode of Action and Results,*" is the title of a new brochure of two hundred pages, published by Drs. Starkey & Palen, which gives to all inquirers full information as to this remarkable curative agent and a record of several hundred surprising cures in a wide range of chronic cases—many of them after being abandoned to die by other physicians. Will be mailed free to any address on application. Read the brochure!

DRS. STARKEY & PALEN,
No. 1529 Arch Street, Philadelphia, Penn.

AND IN CASE YOU RESPOND, STATE WHERE YOU SAW IT.